Invited *is a powerful and prac* take His good news and turn it into your good news. ~...
you will probably recognize yourself in the script. Be ready to understand like never before that having a relationship with Jesus isn't something mystical, but rather very simple. The whole book will bless you, but the built-in reflection questions will help you apply its truths and renew your mind with what God is speaking directly to you. Thanks, Matt, for inspiring us toward intimacy with Jesus in a great way.
—STEVE BACKLUND, FOUNDER OF IGNITING HOPE MINISTRIES

Just occasionally, I read a book that seems to usher me into God's presence. Simple and basic, and even though I've been a follower of Jesus for decades, it awakened in me a hunger to know Jesus more and to go deeper in my spiritual life. I highly recommend it.
—FELICITY DALE, AUTHOR OF AN ARMY OF ORDINARY PEOPLE AND THE BLACK SWAN EFFECT

This book is full of hope and honesty, discovery and discipline, intimacy and intricacy with Jesus. The language used is fresh and stimulating. His illustrations are rich and relevant. The application sections in this book are simple, demonstrating Matt's genius. Consider yourself 'invited' to sit for a spell and be encouraged, refreshed and challenged.
—ED WAKEN, AUTHOR OF WILDFIRE AND PRIMAL FIRE, LEADER OF AN ORGANIC CHURCH NETWORK, AND ADJUNCT PROFESSOR AT GRACE SCHOOL OF THEOLOGY AND ARIZONA CHRISTIAN UNIVERSITY

Matt Berry's book, Invited: A Simple Guide to Connecting with God, *is down to earth, practical, clear and inspirational. It makes God real to anyone, whether they are 'churched' or not. This story is engaging, making it enjoyable to read. As Jesus, this book takes God to the streets, offering to all the opportunity to experience a wonderful loving heavenly father.*
—MARK VIRKLER, FOUNDER OF COMMUNION WITH GOD MINISTRIES AND AUTHOR OF 4 KEYS TO HEARING GOD'S VOICE

Invited is a fresh voice in the conversation about what it means to walk with God and learn to listen and respond as He speaks. Matt Berry's artful yet accessible language appeals to those who haven't grown up in church. Practical and inspiring, this book well earns its merit for those curious about a faith-filled life and those dissatisfied with a dry faith.

–TWYLA FRANZ, THE UNCOMMON NORMAL

Matt has touched what, to many, is a raw nerve–but he's done it in a way which brings hope and healing. So often in life, I've come across people who are desperate to know God, but they don't know HOW to walk with him. Written with colorful stories and personal realism, this book is easy to read and deeply profound. Whether as an affirmation for a seasoned veteran, an encouragement for a journeyman, or an introduction for a seeker, Invited speaks to all of us.

–REV. JOHN D. KOESHALL

Invited was written with you in mind. Matt extends his hand to walk alongside his journey while guiding your thoughts carefully to consider a relationship with the Lord in a new way. Beautifully invitational, don't miss a timely opportunity to refresh your soul. This clear and gentle guide offers helpful spiritual and personal development in a delightful way!

–LISA WELTER, NATIONAL DIRECTOR OF LEADERSHIP DEVELOPMENT, SAFE FAMILIES FOR CHILDREN

Today's culture is plagued with over stimulated complexity and Matt hits a home run on returning faith in Christ to the simple relationship it is supposed to be. He uses many biblical and personal stories while providing thoughtful exercises and action points that serve to move his teachings from conception to doable realities. I will be using this book in discipling new believers as well as seasoned saints… Definitely a book for our times.

–DAVE WEIGEL, PASTOR OF LIVING WATERS CHURCH

A must read for anyone wanting to go deeper and wider with Jesus. This book will motivate you to bring God's kingdom to your everyday life.

–KENNETH BEAUDRY, MIRACLES IN THE MARKETPLACE, AND OWNER OF BEAUDRY OIL & PROPANE

INVITED

MATT BERRY

A SIMPLE GUIDE FOR CONNECTING WITH GOD

Invited: A Simple Guide for Connecting with God
Copyright © 2020 by Matt Berry

No Name Imprints
PO Box 69, 26278 2nd St. E
Zimmerman, MN, 55398
contact@nonameimprints.com

Visit the author's website at www.themattberry.com

ISBN 978-1-7342689-0-4 (paperback)
ISBN 978-1-7342689-1-1 (hardback)
ISBN 978-1-7342689-2-8 (ebook)

Library of Congress Control Number: 2020911747
Dewey Decimal Classification: 248.4
Subject Heading: CHRISTIAN LIFE / CHRISTIAN LIVING

Cover design: Vanessa Maynard
Cover photo: David Charouz/Shutterstock.com
Interior design: Ines Monnet
Interior illustrations: Anne Towner, vectorpouch/Shutterstock.com

Printed in the United States of America.

To my four boys, who have given me gray hairs and interesting content for this book. I wrote the book I wish I could have read when I was your age. It is now here for you. There's no greater joy in life than to discover who you are and whose voice calls out to you, echoing through the caverns of your soul. May Jesus give you grace to reply with little "yeses" every time he calls your name.

TABLE OF CONTENTS

ACKNOWLEDGMENTS

Writing a book is harder than I thought! I half-expected to sit down in front of my laptop and hammer out a draft in a couple of months. I was so naïve. In my mind, it was an exercise of willpower and determination in which I was the only team member. This process has taught me the value of assembling a good team and drawing on their strengths. As John Donne once famously said, "No man is an island entire of itself." It's my joy to now celebrate the contributions others have made to see this book come to print.

I thank my wife, Elisa, who will forever be my "Spanish angel girl." She has been relentlessly supportive, far more confident in me than myself, and keenly aware of how words can be interpreted. She has been God's greatest gift to me on earth. While most of her contributions, her sacrifices, her many "yeses" to Jesus have (to date) never been publicly recognized, I celebrate the ones I have had the honor of seeing. She is gold.

Next comes my parents, Jeff and Krista. Much of what I know about following Jesus came from them. They went "all in" with Jesus in their early adult years, laying a foundation upon which I now stand. They forever changed the course of my family by saying yes to Jesus. Not flashy or flamboyant. They are faithful, steady, and the type of people who endure to the end. By God's grace, I will follow in their footsteps.

Louise Robinson Chapman (1892-1993) comes next. "Grandma" Chapman would invite me over to her house as a young boy, coaxed by a Butterfinger candy bar. She would pray powerful prayers over me. To hear those prayers replayed today! Though I don't recall the words, God remembers them, and I carry something in me today because of her.

And then there's Floyd Dahl (-2018). Floyd was someone I sought out as a young, married man. I'd buy him coffee each week, a small price to pay for the wisdom he shared. He taught me the value of joy and being childlike (not "childish," there's a difference!), and he instilled in me a value for God's Kingdom. The time he spent with me has left an indelible mark on my life. Thanks, "Papa" Floyd.

I also want to thank my team of "beta" readers, who provided me feedback early on. They helped shape the book into what it is today. Thank you, Mary Hedlund, Gene & Betty Keen, Laura Jones, Matt Petz, Justin Cronk, Cody Baragar, William Hannay, Linda Schell. You shared comments like, "This is great!" along with "This is weird." I needed both types of feedback to make these truths relatable and easy to understand.

Thanks also to those who provided endorsements for my book. Their names are printed in the first few pages. They are busy people who took the time to read a "newbie" author like myself. They are also people whose ministries I trust. Check them out.

And lastly, I want to thank *you*, the one reading this book. Time is a precious commodity. I've done my best not to waste your time with needless fluff and filler in this book. Thank you for investing your moments in listening to me as I share about what I have seen and heard.

AUTHOR'S NOTE

As I write this, we're right on the cusp of spring here in Minnesota. There's still snow on the ground, albeit melting, but there has been a noticeable shift in the outdoors. Before too long, tiny seeds will be planted in fertile soil and left under grow lights. For several weeks, what appears to be plain soil will be watered and tended. From our vantage point, nothing will change.

Underneath the soil, however, growth is occurring. Baby roots shoot out from the seed and begin to draw in the water and nutrients from the dirt. The seedling needs a healthy root system to support the growth that will soon erupt and become visible to all.

The inward life of a Jesus follower comprises those things which, for the most part, will go unnoticed by others. The most significant growth takes place in those moments that are hidden from the critique and praise of others. They are the foundations upon which all the outward practices are built.

In this book, I'm going to lay out some foundational practices Jesus modeled while on earth. He lived them out so that we might follow his example. They aren't the *only* ones, but they are very important. I think it best to divide them into two categories.

The inward practices:
- Connection: Nurturing your relationship with God
- Indwelling: Living by the power of God's indwelling Spirit
- Prayer: Seeing and hearing what God is doing

The outward practices:

- Faith: Seeing and believing the truth
- Obedience: The joy, not the burden
- Love: Becoming kindness to all people

As we explore these topics, there will be "pit stops" along the way to reflect on the content. There will be questions to ask, both of yourself and of God. Don't rush through them. This is not the place for half-hearted, fill-in-the-blank responses. Wrestle with the questions. Be honest with yourself. You'll get out of these according to the measure you put in.

At the end of each chapter, there will be opportunities to put into practice what you've chosen to believe. The application section is designed to provide "next steps," combining right thought with purposeful action.

This book has the potential to create momentum in your life. May God give you the grace to respond to Jesus' timeless invitation to follow him.

Matt

Invited: The Digital Journey

I've also developed an online resource to guide you through this material called, *Invited: The Digital Journey*. Each week, you'll receive access to a short video that introduces a chapter in this book. Consider it my way of guiding you through the material. Listen as I share some commentary behind each chapter and give you a glimpse of how I live out these practices in my own life. It's free, but you must sign up at www.themattberry.com/digital-journey.

PREFACE

As we begin our journey together, I feel it's important to share with you a bit about myself. I am an ordinary guy who lives in the Midwest. I mow my lawn on the weekends; that is, so long as there's no snow on the ground here in Minnesota. My wife and I have been married for nearly fifteen years — we have four kids as our witnesses. I work a typical 9-to-5 job and find time to write early in the morning or on my lunch break.

I've never stood on stage at a major conference. To date, my "ministry" has not drawn crowds of thousands or even hundreds. I have no social media following, save a few friends and family who are supporting me in this endeavor. By all popular opinion, these "qualifications" are unimpressive at best. But then again, I've never been one to try to fit in a crowd.

I am like you, or at least *somewhat* like most of you reading this book. I am an average person, writing the lessons in this book, sharing truths that can be practiced by other ordinary people. Consider this a type of *doable* spirituality for those of us who feel neither extraordinary nor particularly brilliant.

Throughout the years, many well-known Christian leaders have had a positive impact on my life. I've listened to their CDs. I've read many of their books. I've even subscribed to a podcast or two. Their contributions have undoubtedly made an impact on my life. Yet, I question whether their lifestyle is at all similar to my own. Theirs feels different from the majority of us who juggle full-time jobs, family, and parenting duties while fighting to find space for the development of our inner selves.

That nagging question eventually turned into an invitation. God spoke to my heart in late 2018, asking, "Would you be willing to write a book?" My response to that question has become what you are now reading today.

This book is a simple guide for connecting with God. For some of you, it may be the first time you've dared to consider the possibility. Or perhaps you may find yourself wanting to reconnect with God, picking up from where you left off earlier in life. Regardless of your point of entry, this book is about connecting with God and nurturing that relationship.

Jesus' invitation first came to men who were fishing along a lakeshore some two thousand years ago. That call is still as relevant and available today as it was back then. It is not only for the 1 percent, those who have exceptional intellects or a knack for spirituality. It is *also* for the remaining 99 percent of us and perhaps *particularly* for those of us who know we're in a place of need (see Mark 2:17).

The invitation of Jesus is simple enough for even a child to answer. It is practical enough for a stay-at-home parent to embrace, even amidst dirty laundry and running errands. It is within reach of someone with a full-time job, struggling to corral the chaos of an overflowing inbox and a day full of meetings. It is an invitation to all.

Jesus said, "Follow me" (Matthew 4:19 ESV). Those words carry just as much weight as they did back when they were first spoken. It is as if he were saying to you, even now: "Come closer. Be near me. Discover who I am and what I think about you. Allow me to reintroduce myself to you."

Although God knows your past in its entirety, both your failures and regrets, he still extends this invitation to you. And the decision you must make, perhaps the *most* important one you'll ever make in life, is this: how will I respond?

FOLLOWING JESUS

1

One way to define spiritual life is getting so tired and fed up with yourself
you go on to something better, which is following Jesus.
—Eugene Peterson

You don't think your way into a new kind of living.
You live your way into a new kind of thinking.
—Henri Nouwen

If we go back to the beginning, to the dusty roads of ancient Israel, there was a man who lived a life so significant that untold millions have shaped their lives around his own. He never traveled more than 200 miles from the place of his birth. He had no social media presence. He was not a blogger, and he never spoke at a conference. He never wrote a book.

Jesus went about his life doing good (Acts 10:38). Ordinary people discovered in him an extraordinary love. He inspired men and women to think differently about God and themselves. His words and actions carried life, springing up out of his inner treasury, which had been developed through a well-nurtured relationship with God, his father.

If you wanted to learn from this man, you couldn't buy his book off Amazon. You couldn't watch his latest docuseries on Netflix. No. To learn from this man, you had to go to where he was. You had to come within earshot of his voice.

Working a long day in the fields, you might return home to learn that Jesus was speaking on a nearby hillside. You grab your spouse and children, put some bread in your bag, and head out the door. Along the journey, you hope to arrive in time to hear what he has to say. Will he offer some words of comfort or wisdom? Will someone be healed miraculously? You would have been walking in excited anticipation to hear this man who people said was unlike anyone you had ever met.

One afternoon, he may be sitting on a hillside. The next day he might be having dinner in the home of some colorful and, perhaps, questionable people — loan sharks, prostitutes, and drug addicts. Still another day, he might walk thirty miles to another town.

But once you heard his voice and his words got stuck in your mind, it would begin to expose the unanswered questions and inner desires of your heart. You wouldn't want to lose his trail. You would follow him wherever he went, no matter the cost.

If you wanted to be more than a casual listener, to be his disciple (literally, his "apprentice"), you had to follow him. And I don't mean merely follow his ideology or intellectually agree with his words as some do today saying, "Amen! That's right!"

You had to add action to your words (See James 2:20). You had to put feet to your faith, strap on your sandals, and follow him wherever he went.

We need to get back to the essence of what it means to follow Jesus.

Come Now, Not Later

There's a story in the Gospel of John about two men who were search-ing for Jesus. They had first followed John the Baptist, who came before, saying, "Prepare the way for the Lord's coming" (Matthew 3:3). It was a logical move. If you don't know who the Savior is, you might as well follow the man whose job it is to prepare his way.

One day, John was standing with two of his disciples as Jesus passed by them. John declared, "Look! There is the Lamb of God!" (John 1:36). The two disciples heard him say this, and they followed Jesus.

I imagine them turning to John and sharing a moment, looking into his eyes. "Thank you for everything. But we can't stay. We have to go. We've found the one for whom we've been searching." John nods in agreement and smiles before saying, "He must increase, but I must decrease" (John 3:30 ESV).

The two men jog down the path to catch up with Jesus. Perhaps he saw them coming or, because he was God, Jesus already knew they were there. I like to imagine they were out of breath, gasping for air after a hard sprint. Their presence was unmistakable.

Turning, he asks them, "What do you want?"

They respond, "Rabbi" (which means "Teacher"), "where are you staying?"

"Come and see," Jesus said (John 1:35-39).

They asked a simple question seeking a direct answer.

Often my prayers are filled with direct questions. I have a habit of interrogating God for answers. Sometimes, I can be a bit rude. I forget about the back-and-forth that happens in a normal conversation. I just rush in with my urgent request: "Lord, I'm in a crisis, and I need an answer right now!"

"Where are you staying?" they asked. Jesus didn't answer their question directly. He didn't give them the answer they sought; otherwise, they might presume to act on it later. Instead, he gave them the answer they needed. He replied with an invitation: "Come, and you will see."

The two men would find their answers only as they walked down the road with Jesus. The truth would be discovered along the journey. "Come now, not later. Come now and walk with me. Respond to my invitation, and you will see."

You Have Been Invited

The life of a Jesus follower begins with and is sustained by responding daily to God's invitation. It is his invitation to you. It is an offer for a deeper, more meaningful relationship. This prospect can feel intimidating. We know ourselves, especially the worst parts we keep hidden from plain view. We ask ourselves, "Will he accept me once he finds out who I really am?

These fears must be calmed. Remember, it is God who calls out to you, not the other way around. He is always the initiator. And since it is his call, you are certainly qualified to respond.

God does not use coercion. God longs to show you his kindness and compassion (Isaiah 30:18). Strong-arm tactics and guilt trips are not his way. But he *is* persistent. He never "slumbers or sleeps" (Psalm 121:4). He waits until the time when you're ready to respond.

To respond to Jesus, all that is required is a simple "Yes." It doesn't matter how small and insignificant it may seem. Bring your "yes," to God and he will take it from there. No formulas, sacred incantations, or multiple-choice exams are required. You are invited, not into a body of knowledge, but into an experience.

Are you already a Christian? You might believe all the things you're supposed to, but something is still missing. You're looking for something fresh. You want something more relevant than a once-a-week spirituality. You want something with substance. This book is a map to guide you and provide encouragement on the road ahead.

> **YOU ARE INVITED, NOT INTO A BODY OF KNOWLEDGE, BUT INTO AN EXPERIENCE.**

Are you on the fence? Others may have misrepresented to you who Jesus is and what he wants. You may have been told he wanted strict conformity to a set of rules with "no questions asked" obedience. This book is going to present a different perspective and I'd be honored if you gave me a chance to tell that story.

Have you been told that your outward behavior is more important than your hidden hurts and nagging questions? In your heart, you're sure they're wrong, but you can't shake the sense that there's still something about this Jesus that is worth pursuing. If so, this book is for you. You're going to discover a Jesus who carries our sorrows (Isaiah 53:4) and is unintimidated by questions or doubt.

Or perhaps you picked up this book out of casual curiosity. "I'm not into the whole Jesus thing, but I'll see what this guy has to say." If that's you, I want to express my thanks for giving me a chance. I'll do my best to not waste your time. It's my hope you'll discover a new perspective on what it means to know Jesus and follow him. The invitation is extended to you.

No matter where you are along the path, Jesus still invites you on the journey and waits for your answer. The surface-level questions you carry, which usually begin with the word "why," may not be immediately answered. In my experience, he rarely answers those questions on command. But the deep-seated questions about your purpose, your value, and your identity — all of those will be explained along the road as you walk with him.

Snowballs and Shortfalls

I have four boys. They're a steady source of joy in my life. Ironically, they can simultaneously keep me young and exhausted. They teach me every day. They've played a tremendous role in teaching me how to follow Jesus in the mundane and in a very practical way.

Last winter, I sent my kids outside to play in the snow. As they headed downstairs, I shouted, "Make sure to wear boots and gloves!" There were a few minutes of rustling and chatter downstairs, and one more warning from me: "Stay away from the sides of the house! Some icicles may fall!"

As the sound of boot steps congregated around the door, I followed it up with one last command: "Be kind to each other, and don't come inside until I call you!" The door slammed. The house was silent — quiet enough to think.

How had I just made outdoor playtime so complicated? They wanted a break from cabin fever, brought on by Minnesota's long winter. There I went and weighed them down with "thou shalt nots." What had happened to me?

I know where it comes from — it's fear. Sure, I could argue that I'm trying to be a good parent by teaching them safety, common sense, and basic courtesy. And, for sure, all those things are good. But if I'm honest with myself, I know these commands come from anxiety. I assume the worst will happen. And I could defend my position quite easily.

Here's the scenario. The older son will lob a snowball that will hit his younger brother. The middle child will pick up a stick and begin breaking icicles, discovering gravity still works as one falls on his head. Crying will ensue. The Crisis Management Team will be deployed — Mom and Dad leading the charge.

In the same way, the Church is guilty of "helicopter parenting" when it comes to spiritual growth. We can be plagued by fear, asking, "What if people get things wrong and deceive themselves?" This is closely followed by rules and regulations: "Thou shalt read thy Bible every day. Thou shalt give money in the offering. Thou shalt not skip Sunday morning services."

Fear creates rules to make up for its lack of trust. It says, "I can't trust you to behave on your own, so I'm going to give you rules to keep your behavior in check." Such an approach communicates, unintentionally or otherwise, that God mostly cares about your outward behavior.

> **FEAR CREATES RULES TO MAKE UP FOR ITS LACK OF TRUST.**

When this fear-based mindset runs the Church, following Jesus becomes hyper-focused on having the right answers, rather than asking the right questions. An undue amount of time is spent collecting the right "facts" about God (how perfect he is), about yourself (how imperfect you are), and about his commands (how closely they must be followed). In this paradigm, Christianity becomes an academic exercise. We end up searching the Scriptures to avoid displeasing God rather than to connect with him — to *know* him.

The other side of the spectrum is disengaged parenting. It's a little too confident that kids know what they should do. It makes too many assumptions, saying, "They'll figure it out." This approach is irresponsible. It fails to provide a framework that positions individuals for success.

The Church has also fallen into this extreme. When this mindset rules the Church, following Jesus becomes a nebulous concept. The Charismatic tradition, of which I am a part, has been guilty of this. The Holy Spirit's guidance has been used as an excuse for not being intentional. "Just trust God to lead you," we exhort. Yes, but even a baby doesn't go from crawling to walking without a lot of oversight from loving and helpful parents.

This approach sets the bar for following Jesus too low. It may be content with praying the sinner's prayer and consistent weekly church attendance, but there is little expectation of movement toward maturity. It often lacks a doable framework to describe in plain terms what it actually means to follow Jesus.

Dietrich Bonhoeffer called this "cheap grace."[1] All are included. All are "disciples," that is, followers of Jesus. Right behavior is welcomed, but also optional. It's like the trend in kids' sports today where everyone gets a trophy just for showing up. "You're all winners," they say, but winners of *what* exactly?

The bar has been set so low that we've tripped over our own good intentions. The exhilarating experience of walking with Jesus, of daily interacting with him and experiencing his joy, is missed. The excitement of discovering how he sees you as a partner with him in life, is left undiscovered.

We need another solution.

Book Nerd to College Dropout

I've always enjoyed understanding how things work. Whenever a toaster or television broke down in my house, I'd be the first to volunteer to dispose of it. Before you applaud me, don't think it was entirely selfless.

Sitting on that cold garage floor, with my dad's tools in hand, gadgets would get broken down into their most essential parts. Meticulous at times, I would remove each screw in sequential order. Occasionally destructive, I'd resort to using a pry bar and hammer. By whatever means necessary, I had to understand what was inside.

It's no surprise that as I grew into a young man, this hobby turned into a foundational way I interacted with the world. I was always probing for answers and was never afraid to tear well-held beliefs apart to understand the underlying "Why?"

As a young man, I was intrigued by the faith of my parents. It was simple, vibrant, and beautifully authentic. It had no air of hypocrisy. Both Mom and Dad were quick to admit failure. I was blessed to see that deep faith in Jesus lived out in the context of ordinary life.

My dad owned a roofing company in Southern California. He would wake up early in the morning to get a jump-start on his day, but not before sitting in the den on his blue La-Z-Boy. He would read the "Our Daily Bread" devotional and pray. Watching my dad, a man who never graduated high school, engage in his faith in such a profound way provoked a curiosity in me no professor ever did. It was something I couldn't shake.

There was substance in his simple faith. It was profound. But where did that substance come from? Why was it so important to him? And what motivated him to wake up at 4:30am every morning when he could be sleeping? These observations fueled my search for answers.

During my high school years, I had an insatiable appetite for reading. I read through the Bible several times, always with pen and highlighter in hand. My birthday and Christmas were often excuses to ask for books and commentaries. I even worked at a Christian bookstore just so I could get the employee discount and be able to pull books off the shelves and read them during my lunch break.

I realize how weird this all sounds so let me just state the obvious: I was a nerdy, Bible-toting, glasses-wearing, fifty-year-old teenager who lived like a monk. I'm so thankful to have *mostly* moved beyond that phase, thanks in no small part to my wife, Elisa. But I was, and will forever be, someone who marches to the beat of my own drum.

In spite of being perhaps the most socially awkward kid in my youth group, all that effort to honestly know and understand God eventually paid off. I had some profound experiences with him. I came to know the feeling where, when reading the Bible, the words would leap off the page and touch my heart. I had encounters where God's presence felt near, almost tangible.

Yet, these experiences were the exception rather than the norm. I was still stumbling in the dark. I knew there was substance out there because I had touched it. Thought at times it had to hit me on the side of my head. But I didn't have a framework or grid to connect with God *consistently*.

There had to be more to this faith than sporadic visitations.

So I did what any wholehearted person would do: I threw myself into the pursuit. I went to college to find my answers. I figured after enough years of education, I would eventually discover the answer to my underlying questions about God. I still thought answers were primarily in books, not in life experience.

College was enjoyable — initially. I loved to learn. Being surrounded by professors and books was the ideal environment for a nerd like me. I took classes on the Old Testament, the Gospels, and New Testament Greek. It was a thrill for me to dive in and gather all this knowledge.

My excitement for learning kept me motivated for the first two semesters. I was accumulating facts that would get peppered into my everyday conversations. "Did you know the books of the Bible aren't organized chronologically? Did you know you should never preach a sermon with more than four points? Did you know that people with leprosy in the Bible might actually have lost their noses due to the disease?"

Looking back, I feel bad for all the conversations I hijacked with useless factoids. College was preparing me to be a pro at Bible trivia, but I wasn't finding the substance I sought. My head was getting big, but my heart was a wasteland. Where was that simple yet profound faith that my parents possessed?

Now in my second year of college, my passion for learning had waned. I remember sitting in my Theology II class, filled with frustration, wondering how much of what the professor taught actually mattered. After all, if all of this were really true — if the gospel was what Jesus said it was — how was what I was learning in a classroom going to impact the way I lived my life? Shouldn't this all be leading us to some sort of dramatic life change rather than just the collection of data points?

I thought about the story in the Book of Acts, where God healed a lame man through Peter and John (see Acts 3). The miracle attracted a crowd, which was made of ordinary people seeking something different, something real. Peter and John were boldly preaching God's good news about the kingdom and the truth about Jesus, and the crowd was witnessing that power in real time as they watched a man regain his ability to walk.

The religious leaders who received news of this were outraged. These fishermen-turned-radicals were challenging the status quo of the religious system. They had kicked the proverbial hornet's nest.

So the authorities arrested them and threw them into jail. The next day, they were brought before the religious leaders to explain themselves. But rather than cowering in shame, Peter gave a defense that the authorities could not deny.

The evidence was hard to ignore. The lame-turned-walking man walked into the room on previously paralyzed legs and gave proof of his healing. He was known throughout the community. Even the most vocal critics couldn't deny that something miraculous had occurred.

Peter and John were released. What else could their critics do?

But here's the part of that story that captivated me, even as the professor continued his bland lecture in the background. "Now when they [the critics] saw the boldness of Peter and John and perceived that they were uneducated, common men, they were astonished. And they recognized that they had been with Jesus" (Acts 4:13 ESV).

These men had followed Jesus in the most literal sense, from town to town, for over three years. They had lived next to him. They had laughed with him. They knew him more profoundly than any textbook could describe. And now they were doing the things Jesus did. How remarkable!

Peter and John were "uneducated, common men," like many of us. They weren't professional ministers. They hadn't gone to Bible college or seminary. Their lack of book knowledge had not disqualified them from being used by God.

Peter and John were filled with boldness. They had encountered something of substance in Jesus that had transferred to them.

THEIR LACK OF BOOK KNOWLEDGE HAD NOT DISQUALIFIED THEM FROM BEING USED BY GOD.

His life infected them like a virus, and the outbreak was unstoppable. They were filled with the confidence and desire to share Jesus' life-altering message with others, not only with words, but also with power (1 John 3:18).

I looked around my classroom and saw young men and women who were very much like myself. They were struggling with doubt, not knowing who they were, and hoping to God that this pricey college degree would give them answers.

"They recognized that they had been with Jesus."

Would anyone know today, if they had to guess, whether you had been in touch with Jesus? Has the quality of your following been such that Jesus' essence has rubbed off on you?

It was in that classroom that I made a bold decision. I decided to drop out of school. The answers I sought would not be found by sitting at a desk.

For a book nerd like me to just leave school? The horror! My risky decision turned quite a few heads.

It was a liberating feeling to walk off the campus, not knowing the road that was ahead. It was full of uncertainty, yes. It was entirely incongruent with common sense. However, I had the inner conviction that I was following Jesus off the campus.

A NOTE TO THE READER:

Some of you, particularly those who are considering higher education or are in school currently, may be tempted to make my story your own. Don't drop out of school just because I did. We will cover the mechanics of hearing God's voice in a subsequent chapter. For now, understand that each person has their own path to follow. We aren't all given the same invitation to follow Jesus. For me, it led away from formal education for a season. I did return, though not to the same school. For others, however, it may lead only deeper into formal training, and there is nothing wrong with that.

The challenge, frustration, even the uniqueness of a life of following Jesus, is that he doesn't lead any two people down the exact same path. He will show you the way if you're willing to follow.

Follow the Leader

The guiding principle for this book Is found In 1 John 2:6: "Whoever says he abides in him ought to walk in the same way in which he walked" (ESV). There's another version that I like for its simplicity. It may resonate more with you. "Those who say they live in God should live their lives as Jesus did".

In the early days, you had to remain close to Jesus to be his disciple. They followed in his footsteps — not just intellectually, but holistically.

They were quite literally on the road with him, traveling from place to place. A choice had to be made — sometimes a costly one, but always an intentional one — to be with him and to remain connected to him.

Scripture doesn't tell us to simply believe the right things; it challenges us to model our lives, our daily and sometimes very mundane decisions, after the example given to us by Jesus.

Let me ask you a question. How did you learn to tie your shoes? Did you pour over textbooks and reference books? Did you attend a seminar? Maybe you paid someone with a degree to educate you on the proper and improper methods of tying laces. I would wager you learned how to tie your shoes by watching someone show you how it was done.

We learn best when we can first see it modeled for us. Some might be audacious enough to call this the "fake it 'til you make it" approach. I prefer to call it the "practice it 'til you become it" principle.

When it comes to a lifestyle of following Jesus, his guidance is quite simple: Come to me, see how I live, and follow my example. The invitation is extended to all but is always delivered personally. At times it may have been hidden, shining underneath a steaming pile of ideological baggage and misrepresentation, but its core message has remained the same.

He extends the same call to us as he did to the disciples along the lakeshore so long ago, "Come, follow me..." (Matthew 4:19 ESV).

> **SOME MIGHT BE AUDACIOUS ENOUGH TO CALL THIS THE "FAKE IT 'TIL YOU MAKE IT" APPROACH. I PREFER TO CALL IT THE "PRACTICE IT 'TIL YOU BECOME IT" PRINCIPLE.**

Through the Lens of Jesus

If you were to close your eyes right now and picture God looking at you, what would be the expression on his face? Would he be preoccupied with something else? Would he be frustrated, maybe even a bit angry? I used to think of God in those terms. Each failure was just another reminder of how much of a disappointment I was to him — or so I thought.

A.W. Tozer said it best: "What comes into our minds when we think about God is the most important thing about us."[2] It contributes significantly to our identity. If an all-powerful being exists — and he knows who we are — then what does he want out of us? What are his expectations?

We find these answers in Jesus. He is the most accurate expression of what God is like. Scripture says he "is the radiance of [Father] God's glory and the exact representation of his nature" (Hebrews 1:3 NASB). The word for "representation" there is *charaktér*, from which we get the word "character." It literally means "an imprint." It's a word picture based on how coins were produced at that time. A small piece of metal would be formed and then stamped with an image. The face or *charaktér* of the Roman emperor would be imprinted on the coin.

You will never see God more clearly than in the face of Jesus. He came to earth to address that question once and for all. Every story of God in the Bible has to be read through the lens of Jesus — what he said and how he lived. Every other approach will end in disappointment.

When I came to believe this about Jesus, my perspective dramatically changed. It was an injection of hope into my weary soul. His reactions to people, recorded in the Gospels, connected me with the heart of the God I so desperately wanted to know. I discovered his default emotional state toward me was not anger and frustration, but rather extravagant kindness and compassion.

I began reading myself into these Gospel stories. It was I who was the prostitute in John 8, standing condemned by my accusers, covered in the shame of my own shortcomings. But instead of receiving judgment, I heard his words, "Neither do I condemn you; go, and from now on sin no more" (John 8:11 ESV).

It was I, not only Zacchaeus, who climbed the sycamore tree in Luke 19. I had to get a glimpse, even if just for a moment, of Jesus. My love for him was small, but it was real. And instead of being passed by as just another bystander, I encountered Jesus' joyful expression and heard his welcoming voice shout, "Quick, come down! I must be a guest in your home today" (Luke 19:5).

When we have an accurate point of entry to approach God, we find ourselves welcomed into his presence, never rejected. We are invited by name, never overlooked. We are qualified for connection with him, not held in limbo until our lives looks presentable. He says, "Come to me just as you are."

This offer is presented to us, again and again, until we finally come to believe that his invitation is genuine. He really wants us. Not out of obligation. Not because his character requires it. We are wanted, significant, and invited to join him on the journey — to be his disciples, his followers.

A New Way to Be Human

When Jesus walked the earth, he was just like us. The Apostle John explained it this way: "The Word became flesh and blood and moved into the neighborhood. We saw the glory with our own eyes, the one-of-a-kind glory, like Father, like Son, generous inside and out, true from start to finish" (John 1:14 MSG).

God became a man. He stepped into our existence, took on our limitations, and modeled for us what it looks like to be human — in the most real sense of the word.

He knows what it's like to work a full-time job. He was a carpenter before there were power tools and Ford F-150s and Home Depots upon which to rely. He knows the struggle of feeling tired, juggling responsibilities, and running out of hours in the day.

He knows what it's like to lose someone you love. By the time Jesus was thirty, his adopted father, Joseph, was no longer mentioned. Most scholars believe he died during Jesus' childhood. Imagine needing to step in and provide for your grieving mother.

He can relate to us. As it says in Hebrews, he "understands our weaknesses, for he faced all of the same testing we do" (Hebrews 4:15). No one understands more than Jesus just how challenging life can be.

While he can (and does) relate to me, I can also relate to him. This is where his invitation to "follow me" takes on a deeper meaning. It becomes a call to which I can respond.

The life of Jesus becomes a blueprint for us to follow. He shows us how to live the Christian life in full dependence on the Father. His actions were made significant by the life of the Father, who was within him. This is our example, and it gives us hope that we can respond to his invitation.

If Jesus did it, so can you. But don't just take my word for it. Listen to what Jesus himself says: "Truly, truly, I say to you, whoever believes in me will also do the works that I do, and greater works than these will he do…" (John 14:12 ESV).

A few years back, on a warm summer afternoon, my son Judah asked if I could teach him how to mow the lawn. Now, entrusting your seven-year-old child with a gas-powered, self-propelled lawn mower carries with it enough worst-case scenarios to make any responsible parent say no.

In fact, I did say no several times. All these "what ifs" played across the screen of my mind's imagination. Little boy's feet are meant to stay attached to little boy's legs. I wanted to be careful not to put him in a situation where he could fail beyond recovery.

At that age, he wasn't yet ready to mow the lawn solo, but I invited him to "help" me by placing his little hands on the handles, right next to mine. As I pushed the mower back and forth across the lawn, Judah partnered with me. His primary job was to walk with me and to watch how I handled the mower.

He learned to mow the grass by seeing it modeled right in front of him. He was protected throughout the learning process. His father's watchful eye oversaw every detail and guarded against every slip or misstep.

Since then, we've moved to the country. Our yard is much bigger than the little city plot we had back in Saint Paul. And guess who operates the push mower? My boy. He mows the area around each tree as I cut back and forth across our acreage with the big riding lawn mower.

He's grown up and become my partner. We work together and exchange smiles and thumbs up throughout the process. He's learned how to "be about his father's business" (Luke 2:49 ESV).

The same is true for our spiritual growth. Jesus came to show us what it looks like to be fully human. He laid aside his abilities and took on the weakness of our human existence (Philippians 2:5). While on earth, he modeled how to live an extraordinary life in spite of the flaws and shortcomings with which we are so acquainted.

Like a son learning how to mow the lawn with his father, Jesus invites men and women to follow his example and to partner with him. We are invited to watch and learn from him firsthand.

I'm convinced that we will experience the results Jesus had if we live the way Jesus lived. It's worth repeating. "Truly, truly, I say to you, whoever believes in me will also do the works that I do, and greater works than these will he do…" (John 14:12 ESV). We need to reimagine what a life can look like when it is lived the way God designed it.

A different way of life is laid before us, modeled by Jesus, who is both our God (Philippians 2:6) and

WE NEED TO REIMAGINE WHAT A LIFE CAN LOOK LIKE WHEN IT IS LIVED THE WAY GOD DESIGNED IT.

our brother (Hebrews 2:11). It's time for us to believe that we are meant for greater things. This journey is not one of striving, where we muster up our strength, pulling up our proverbial boots by their bootstraps. Instead, it's a way propelled by the life of Jesus, made possible through a relationship with him.

As we follow in his footsteps, we'll discover the wind at our backs and the Spirit of God at work in our souls, bringing light to dark places and challenging us to see ourselves as meant for greater things.

CONNECTION:
Nurturing Your Relationship with God

2

To fall in love with God is the greatest romance;
to seek him, the greatest adventure; to find him, the greatest achievement.
–St. Augustine

You were made by God and for God
and until you understand that life will never make sense.
–Rick Warren

The winters in Minnesota can be long and relentlessly cold, especially toward the end of the season. My kids get restless. It's called "cabin fever." They have to find some outlet for all their pent-up energy. Otherwise, whining and brotherly spats become the soundtrack for the day. In a proactive move, my wife signed all four boys up for swimming lessons at the local high school.

The Berry family arrives at the pool, loaded with bags of clean clothes, snacks, and water bottles. If it seems we're prepared, you're right. We're professionals. Pre-swim showers? Check. Goggles? Found and adjusted. The teachers signal for the kids to jump into the water. At last, they're off.

We breathe a sigh of relief.

My wife and I sit atop the bleachers, overlooking the pool. We chat about our day, but mostly we just enjoy the silence. After feverishly getting the Berry boys from point A to Z, it feels nice to "flip the switch" and just to be present in the moment.

My eyes scan the pool, looking for each of my boys. Each is unique. Noah swims like a fish, sometimes forgetting he even has an instructor. My oldest son, Judah, is intent to learn every lesson completely — and get it right the first time. He's just like his dad. Then there's Zach, our talkative one. He's more excited to unleash a flood of constant questions and comments at his teacher than to swim.

And then there's the baby of the bunch, our five-year-old Micah. From atop the bleachers, I look down and see him. He's bobbing up and down in the water. His face is full of joy. No one needs to teach this boy how to slow down and be in the moment. He's laughing. He's in his element.

Then it happens.

From across the pool complex, his bright blue eyes look up at me. We lock eyes, and he reveals a bright, half-toothy smile. He waves expressively overhead. He's been waiting for me to notice.

As he looks at me, my heart is undone. It becomes a puddle on the bleacher steps.

Here I am, suspended at this moment and, quite honestly, not wanting to move on. However, Micah *does* have a swimming lesson, so he turns his gaze back to the teacher. He begins to focus on his bobs and learning to hold his breath underwater.

Life moves on for Micah, but not me. That one brief point of connection has left me wanting more. Nothing is more important at this moment than him.

From that point on, I am always watching him. I am anticipating every move, hoping that it will be the one that causes his eyes to look back toward mine.

At that moment, I am reminded of my most important and sacred responsibility as a father. It's not to provide food and clothing. Neither is it to give advice and guidance. All those things are good, but they pale in comparison to one thing: valuing the relationship I have with them. That is, being intentional to nurture the connectedness I have with my boys.

Jesus once said, "If you sinful people know how to give good gifts to your children, how much more will your heavenly Father give good gifts to those who ask him" (Matthew 7:11). He's making an important point. God is an even better father than you on your best day.

Have you ever considered that, like a father on the bleachers watching his son in the pool, God is watching and waiting for you to look at him? He's waiting for the moment where you turn your attention toward him, not to get something, but just to enjoy the shared connection. What a thought to consider! God is waiting for you.

God, the Father of all fathers, lives for the moments when you turn toward him. When you look in his direction, albeit weak, insecure, and highly-distractible, his heart is moved. Have you ever considered the idea that you move God's heart?

This truth can be challenging to accept. You may not have had a father in your life growing up, or, worse, you might have had a father who didn't embody the love and affection you deserved. Either way, we tend to define God's love for us in terms of the love our biological or adopted father modeled toward us. And sometimes that model isn't a good one.

It can be hard to believe that God's love is more than our own experience. But at this moment, I am challenging you to doubt your doubts.

He wants you to be confident in his love like Micah was that day in the pool. And to get to that point, he's provided an example for us to follow.

He's Better Than You Think

Jesus is our blueprint for what it looks like to live a normal human life. That is not a typo. Though fully God, Jesus took on our humanity in its entirety. He lived a life, just like our own, but with a healthy relationship with God the Father, and so he modeled a lifestyle which you and I can follow.

We are invited to follow him, but into what exactly? Do we follow him into overseas missions? Perhaps he requires some extraordinary type of lifestyle? Does he want us to adopt a different set of ethics? Must we take a vow of poverty? What does it practically look like to follow him?

If you spend any length of time reading the Gospels, you'll notice that Jesus talked about his Father more than anything. In the Gospel of John alone, Jesus mentions his Father 120 times.

When speaking about eternal life, Jesus said, "And *this* is eternal life, that they *know* you, the only true God, and Jesus Christ whom you have sent" (John 17:3 ESV). Jesus describes eternal life not as a function ("What will I do?") but as a relationship ("Who do I know?").

His life was built upon a confident expectation of his Father's love. It was foundational and, I believe, the source from which everything else flowed. There was nothing more important to Jesus than being connected to his Father.

> **JESUS DESCRIBES ETERNAL LIFE NOT AS A FUNCTION ("WHAT WILL I DO?") BUT AS A RELATIONSHIP ("WHO DO I KNOW?").**

This quality of knowing is more than simply acknowledging a fact. And yet, isn't that what Christianity has become to some people? It's a verbal nod in the direction of a generalized truth: "I know. I know." Many in the Western world are familiar with the imagery of a man nailed to a cross. We've seen the WWJD (What Would Jesus Do?) bracelets. We sing songs around Christmastime: "Joy to the world! The Lord has come. Let earth receive her king!" And yet, we're still left empty. Our faith must be more than chorus lines, slogans, and head knowledge.

What does eternal life mean to you? As a kid, I remember languishing at the idea of heaven: sitting on a cloud for all eternity, harp in hand, singing the same songs over and over. The monotony of this picture still makes me cringe. This is what I thought heaven looked like.

But Jesus paints a different image and invites us into its reality.

The quality of "knowing" God has been lost in translation. The original language expresses "knowing" in intimate terms. It's like the closeness that a husband and wife treasure or what you might share with a very close friend or family member. I'll give you an example.

My wife and I often complete each other's sentences. "I'm wondering if we should…" I say, my voice trailing off as I'm caught deep in thought. To which my wife, Elisa, responds, "Yeah, it probably would be a good idea to give him a call." How did she know what I was thinking?

No, my wife can't read my mind. Still, our years of shared experiences have allowed her to read between the lines and understand what I'm trying to express even before I finish my sentence. We didn't come into that closeness and understanding by accident. It was developed by spending time together and letting her into my world so that she might understand me on a deeper level.

Similarly, life with God is about relationship and vulnerability. Accepting the invitation becomes an entry point into a lifelong journey, one of being deeply known and scandalously accepted.

This requires a shift in the way we think about God.

This world system has programmed us to view ourselves in terms of what we produce and, therefore, possess. "What do you do for work? What brand of car do you drive? Where do you live?" This sick game forces some to work harder to keep up appearances. Others simply give up. Some even give up on life itself.

When God is approached from that failed mindset, it's easy to come to him asking, "What do you want from me?" We can ask the question as if our value could be defined in the same terms as the world's system. Left unchecked, even the best of us can fall into this mindset and think of ourselves as being nothing more than servants.

We would do well to remind ourselves often of his words spoken through the prophet Isaiah, "My thoughts are nothing like your thoughts... and my ways are far beyond anything you could imagine" (Isaiah 55:8). Don't assume he thinks like you. Even if he had a bad day — and he doesn't — his worst thought would be too mind-blowing for you to comprehend.

What are we called instead? "No longer do I call you servants, for the servant does not know what his master is doing; but I have called you friends..." (John 15:15 ESV).

His words are just as valid today as they were then. If you have been called a friend, never settle for anything less. Our relationship is not transactional. We are not servants.

Jesus came to reveal the Father to us. "Anyone who has seen me has seen the Father!" (John 14:9). All our doubt-filled dissonance about God's kindness and goodness is resolved in the person of Jesus Christ.

Just as I was watching my son at the swimming pool, God is saying, "I've been sitting on the bleachers watching you, just waiting for the moment when your eyes would look up at mine. You've been busy swimming around the pool, learning your bobs, and how to hold your breath underwater. You have been distracted by the busyness of life around you. Yet all this time, I've been waiting for the moment when you'd look at me and discover how much I love you."

What a remarkable thing it is to be wanted! To be wanted, not based on what you have but on who it is that loves you. Along with this invitation comes the revelation that you have value. Perhaps you never knew it. It was hidden deep within, underneath the weaknesses and shortcomings we're all so prone to focus on. So be brave. Doubt your doubts and dare to believe that you're wanted far more than you ever considered possible.

Living for God's Love

You might be sitting here thinking, "I'm quite surprised — and a little embarrassed — that God sees something of value in me. But what now? What does it look to respond to such an invitation?"

Again, we need to shift our focus back to Jesus. Not only does he show us what God is like, but he also models what it looks like for a normal human being to respond to that invitation and live within that love. His life becomes our model.

Let's journey back to the beginning of Jesus' ministry, long before he had healed the lepers, driven out demons, and preached his famous Sermon on the Mount. Let's go way back to the beginning when Jesus was just Mary's son, an ordinary, working-class person like you or me.

Jesus had a cousin, John, who was one of those guys who never drew inside the lines as a child. He was a nonconformist, a rebel to some, always questioning the status quo. John the Baptist came into public view before Jesus. His message was fiery: "Repent!" In our words, "Turn from how you've been living!" He was a catalyst for change and a man of action. John was my kind of guy. "The time has come to choose sides. There's no fence to straddle!"

John came declaring the kingdom of God had nearly arrived. He was the advance team, preparing the way for the Lord. The people of ancient Israel were filled with heightened expectancy. His message instilled hope that something else, something better, was fast approaching.

John didn't look quite like what you might expect as a harbinger of the Messiah. He was wearing camel-hair clothes that never saw a washing machine or bar of soap. There was definitely an odor that followed him, and his beard was disheveled. But despite all this, his eyes were filled with passion and purpose.

The religious leaders — hypocrites, elitists, hungry for control — were all terrified. John questioned the status quo, and squarely placed a target on their backs. They were the ones standing in the way of the coming kingdom. The ordinary people, however, those who were longing for something better, found this message of the coming Messiah to be the water their thirsty hearts wanted.

Crowds made the long, dusty journey into the wilderness to hear John's message along the Jordan River. This was over twenty miles east of Jerusalem. In the middle of nowhere, beyond all their comforts, they came to be baptized in water. It was a sign of their commitment to this coming kingdom.

One day, John was interrupted as he spoke to the crowds. His eyes singled out one man from among the people. It was someone he had not expected. It was Jesus, and he had come to be baptized. Though John tried to talk him out of it, the matter had already been settled. Jesus joined John in the waters of the Jordan River, and there he was baptized.

This Jesus hadn't done a single miracle up until this point to prove himself, yet he heard a voice from heaven saying, "This is my dearly loved Son who brings me great joy" (Matthew 3:16-17).

All the people there along the Jordan River heard the voice. His qualification from the throne of heaven came in the form of a blessing. Having not yet delivered any great sermons or performed any miracles, this Jesus received praise and affirmation from his Father. The Father saw his son as a source of great joy. What a demonstration of the value of relationship!

Jesus received his stamp of approval based on his Father's love.

The relationship with the Father is what Jesus spoke about and from which he taught and performed miracles. It was his source of identity and the goal of his ministry. He revealed the heart of the Father to everyone he spoke to, everyone he healed, everyone he delivered.

"The Father loves the Son and has given all things into his hand" (John 3:35 ESV). Love was the qualification and the source of his authority.

In the words of Jack Frost, "You teach what you know… but impart who you are." Jesus was, first and foremost, a "much-loved son" of the Father who had been "marked" (that is, defined) by this love. It was foundational to his identity.

Because he held to this defining truth in his life, that is, "I am the delight of my Father," he was able to impart it to the people around him. He invited others into the same reality. His mission was to reveal the heart of the Father and his desire for relationship to everyone he encountered. It didn't matter their social status, their wealth, or how messed up their life was. He announced, "You are loved by my Father" to everyone he met.

How comfortable are you with the idea that God the Father loves you? Perhaps at a surface level, you have come to believe that concept. It *is* in the Bible, after all. And a good Christian ought to trust what the Bible says, right?

It's possible to believe in God's love but live life in perpetual shame or condemnation. That's because it's one thing to accept a fact, but it's something entirely different to live *into* that truth. It must still take root in the fabric of your life. Truth must affect the way you see yourself. Until then, it's just another fact to be forgotten.

Failure Before Freedom

In the last chapter, I shared how I dropped out of school. My frustration had reached a tipping point. I wasn't finding the answers I needed in books and lectures. My professors could only offer me the theory — I needed something practical. Where could I get my hands dirty? I decided to leave the comfort of the Kansas City suburbs, join Youth With A Mission (YWAM), and fly to literally the other side of the planet.

So I went to India. There I served orphans in some of the most impoverished places on earth. I taught English in rural villages in the Himalayan mountains. It was a phenomenal experience. I was finally doing something that seemed relevant. However, after the initial excitement wore off, I realized something was still missing.

My actions may have seemed impressive outwardly, but within I battled troubling thoughts: *Shouldn't I have discovered my answers by now? How much longer will God remain patient with me? I've taken too long.* These negative thoughts held me captive. I didn't find my answers in India.

Instead, I saw myself as a disappointment and assumed God was frustrated with me.

I'm not Jesus, after all. He was perfect. That's why the Father could so whole-heartedly love him. But not me. This was my lament — that I was not good enough. Sometimes, albeit briefly, I'd perform some virtuous act that, in my wrong thinking, would bring a half-smile to God's face. But the satisfaction would disappear, stolen away by my own hidden struggles with pornography, body image, and self-hatred.

In my despair, I saw God as an emotionally distant father who was mostly preoccupied with more pressing matters. He saved me and brought me into his family, but I could only see myself as a second-class son — the runt of the litter. In my worst moments, I imagined a sour glare on his face. As if he were looking down in frustration, thinking to himself, "I sent my Son to die for you, to wash away your sins, and *this* is how you repay me? *This* is how you repay the great gift that I gave to you?"

Neither my Bible college education nor overseas experience could deliver me from this inward hell. My mind knew the right answers, but my heart couldn't accept them. I didn't *feel* loved. I felt dirty and broken. I believed God was good, and I loved Jesus, but I couldn't grasp that he felt the same about me.

While my journey didn't produce answers, it did shed light on a mistruth that had poisoned the well of my thoughts and actions. I had a faulty understanding of God's heart, which in turn caused me to draw incorrect conclusions about myself. My experience was far from the standard that Jesus modeled. He talked about God the Father differently. Their relationship was his source of strength, not condemnation. Something had to change, and God, unbeknownst to me, was already working out a plan for my freedom.

God Got Dirty

After I returned from India, I felt lost. My around-the-world trip didn't end how I expected it to. So I did what most people do when they feel lost: I went back to what I knew. I decided to find a college where I could finish up my college degree. If nothing else, I was checking a box on my journey to adulthood.

I found a school far away in Minnesota called Bethany College of Missions (now Bethany Global University). This school was more affordable than most, plus they placed value on applying what was taught. It seemed like a good fit, though I wasn't too keen on the mandatory chapel services held throughout the week. Who likes feeling pressured to go to church? Not this guy. There was no shortage of critical remarks muttered beneath my breath.

On one occasion, a guest speaker visited the college. Allen Hood, from the International House of Prayer in Kansas City, was going to speak about "intimacy" with God. That sounded weird. Services were going to be held twice a day for the entire week. As you can imagine, that did not go over well with me and my cynical attitude.

They want me to be in the service? I said to myself. *Fine! I'll be in the building, but I'm not going to sit in the pews with all the rest of the students.* So I snuck upstairs into a dark, quiet room with a big picture window that overlooked the sanctuary. I sat down in a rocking chair, folded my arms across my chest, and let out a sigh. The preacher stood up to speak. *Here we go,* I thought. I imagine God let out a chuckle. Unbeknownst to me, his perfect ambush had been set.

The preacher began by reading a passage from the beginning of Genesis, which described how God created the world. He read, "And God said, 'Let there be light,' and there was light" (Genesis 1:3 ESV).

With just a few words, God called life into being. Nature and science responded to the sound of his voice. I had read this story a hundred times, but it was as if I was hearing it for the first time. Was it the Southern drawl of this preacher's voice, or was the story crossing that 100-mile distance between my head and my heart?

The preacher continued: "Everything God spoke into existence. That is, except for one — human beings. When he made Adam, the first man, he rolled up his sleeves and got his hands dirty."

Here was a picture of God that I had never considered, a god who was not bothered by dirt. He chose to create that way. The potential for a mess did not turn him away, even if he would get dirt underneath his fingernails. He got involved personally. It wasn't an inconvenience when God made people. Frustration was not on his mind that day, but rather the joy-filled pursuit of making something and calling it "good" (Genesis 1:31).

I saw myself as Adam, in need of formation and identity. He wasn't repelled by my brokenness. It's not as if he were a young child, screaming at the sight of an "icky" spider crawling on the ground. He didn't need to shield his holy gaze from the wreck of a person in front of him.

I knelt on the ground in that darkened room, and I wept. Big, salty tears fell down my face, burning as they came out. I had come into that room all alone, but now I felt surrounded by God's presence. He had come to change my heart.

For the first time, I saw in my mind's eye a picture of God as my father, pulling me close to him and embracing me. He *actually* saw past my failures and found something in me worth loving. God engineered this encounter to show me firsthand that he was not frustrated and emotionally distant. Instead, he loved me enough to chase me down when I wasn't expecting it and to meet me where I was at, hidden away in that upstairs room.

Made for Something More

The preacher continued, "Where did God place man after he created him? That's right, he placed him in a garden." He explained how, in ancient times, gardens were the prized possession of the rich and powerful. Into these walled enclosures, the most beautiful fruit trees would be planted. They would provide pleasure to the taste buds. The rarest birds would be brought in to please the ears with their singing. Beautiful plants and animals would delight the eyes. A garden was designed to bring pleasure to the senses. A garden was a place of encounter.

God placed the first people in this garden. They were told to tend and watch over it. This may sound like a massive act of labor, except for the fact that the garden watered itself and had no weeds (Genesis 2:6 and Genesis 3:18). So what were they to do in a self-sustaining garden?

Adam and Even were created for an encounter. They were designed to absorb the pleasure in that place, brought on by the sights and sounds and tastes around them. And when the cool breeze of the evening would come, so too would the presence of God arrive. And God would walk with them.

They weren't created to be servants. This is unlike creation stories from other religions, where people become slaves to feed the gods and to build their

I HAD BEEN WORKING SO HARD TO EARN THE LOVE AND ACCEPTANCE I ALREADY HAD.

temples. Adam and Eve weren't created to fill some unmet need of God. Instead, they were made for a relationship — designed by God *for* God himself. He wanted to know them and be known by them.

This revelation shattered the false understanding I had about myself. It was a lightbulb moment. I realized I wasn't destined to be just another unworthy servant. His interest in me was not based on a projected rate of return. Instead, my identity was so much more amazing than I had been willing to accept. I had been working so hard to earn the love and acceptance I already had.

While my mom may say I decided to follow Jesus when I was five, I felt as if I were born again that day in the chapel. It was on that day I accepted my true identity and value to God. I "prayed the prayer" when I was five, but in that upper room, something changed within me. I decided to accept the reality that I was designed to know God and be known by him. God wanted to know me as a friend and not just as a servant. And that decision changed everything.

Reflect

Setting aside time to reflect allows us to become more aware of our inner selves and what God may be showing us. It's like a shopping mall directory, searching for the "You are here" arrow. Reflection helps us to understand where we are and where we want to go.

Allow your heart and mind to think about and process what we covered thus far, paying attention to your inner feelings, questions, and even frustrations. During reflection, we create space for God to search our hearts and expose things that were previously hidden. This results in an authentic connection, both with God and ourselves.

- Up until this point, how have you related to God? If you had to describe his emotions toward you, would they be warm and affectionate? Would they be cold, distant, or frustrated? It may help to close your eyes and visualize what you think God's expression would be if he were looking at you. Write down your notes in the space below.

_____

_____

_____

_____

_____

_____

- When you're feeling your worst, do you run toward God or away from him? Is allowing yourself to be deeply known by him hard to consider? If so, why do you think that is?

_____

_____

_____

_____

_____

_____

- Take a moment to think about how you live your life. Do you relate to God more as a servant or as a friend? Is it difficult to believe you were created for connection?

_____

_____

_____

_____

_____

_____

_____

_____

- How might your life look different if you fully embraced God's love and attitude toward you, as described in this chapter? What would be one noticeable change in the way you lived? What is one thing that others might notice about you were you to believe these truths?

_____

_____

_____

_____

_____

_____

_____

_____

Dare to Believe

Jesus believed his Father enjoyed him. For those of us who would follow in his footsteps, we are given the same invitation to respond to that love. In John 17, Jesus is once again in dialogue with the Father.

"I have given them the glory you gave me, so they may be one as we are one. I am in them and you are in me. May they experience such perfect unity that the world will know that you sent me and that *you love them as much as you love me*." (John 17:22–23, emphasis mine).

Did you catch the last phrase? "And loved them even as you loved me." These words were difficult to accept when I first read them. How is it possible that the Father could love me in the same way he loved Jesus? To even consider the idea was outside my comfort zone. It felt as though it teetered on the brink of blasphemy. How could it be possible that the Father could love me with the same quality of love that he had for his own son?

I remember one day, as I pondered this, the Father spoke to my heart and told me, "I don't have any second-rate sons."

God doesn't just possess love; he *is* love. To come in contact with God is to touch love in its purest form. He can't express less than one hundred percent. "Love never gives up, never loses faith, is always hopeful, and endures through every circumstance" (1 Corinthians 13:7). This means he doesn't have "off days" where his love for you wanes. Will you believe it?

This concept was revolutionary — and uncomfortable. It took courage to change my paradigm and allow this scandalous truth to take root inside my heart. I accepted it cautiously, kind of like touching a pot on the stove, not knowing whether it's hot.

Tap, tap. "Can I touch it?" Touch it a little longer. "Okay, I can touch it. It's safe." It was a process for me to accept that love.

The value of something is determined by what you'll pay to get it. Consider how Jesus died on the cross. Imagine the suffering involved in that act of obedience. Now ponder how Jesus *willingly* embraced that path. Why? Because of "the joy set before him" (Hebrews 12:2). *You* were his prize.

You were so valuable to the Father that he gave what was most precious to him, Jesus, to bring you close to himself. That's why the Church throughout history has called this "the gospel," which means "good news." This is not good news in a generic sense; it's deeply personal. This is good news *for you*. Will you dare to believe it?

In the words of C.S. Lewis, "Do not dare not to dare."

There are times when you have to step outside your comfort zone and, by faith, accept the truth even when it seems too scandalous to believe.

Dare to allow yourself to be loved by God. Dare to believe that you were created for encounter. You may not feel worthy. Good! You don't need to be. In fact, none of us are worthy of such love. But don't let that stop you from receiving the best news you'll ever receive: You are precious to God.

Hidden Growth

One of my favorite children's stories is "The Garden" from Arnold Lobel's book of stories titled *Frog and Toad Together*. It's a tale about two friends with very different viewpoints.

Frog is the optimistic one. For our slimy friend, the glass is always at least half full. He's never too busy or distracted to enjoy the small things in life. Worry and discouragement are strangers to this happy fellow.

Toad, on the other hand. Oh, miserable Mr. Toad. He struggles to see things in a positive light. He's our pessimist, prone to despair, quick to give up, and he takes himself far too seriously. Fortunately for him, he has Frog as his best friend.

One day, Toad comes to visit Frog. His friend is working in the garden. He leans on the fence, admiring the flowers his friend has grown: beautiful white daisies with yellow centers, as large as his head.

"I wish I had a garden," says Toad.

"Here are some flower seeds," says Frog. "Plant them in the ground, and soon you will have a garden."

"How soon?" asks Toad.

"Quite soon," says Frog.

Toad hops home and plants the seeds. He wipes the dirt off his hands, paces back and forth a few times, and laments at the lack of growth.

"Now seeds, start growing!" he commands.

I chuckle every time I read this story. Miserable Mr. Toad needs some sage advice from his friend: Growth occurs over the long haul. It's often slow, and most of it is often hidden from plain view.

Responding to the Father's love is like gardening. Our dear helper, the Holy Spirit, is like Mr. Frog in the story. He's always looking on the bright side of life. He's present amid our struggles and ready to help. "Here are some flower seeds," he

> **"HOW SOON?" ASKS TOAD. "QUITE SOON," SAYS FROG.**

says. The seeds are the beginnings of a connected life with the Father. They're a gift that must be planted, watered, and given time to grow.

There will be seasons when explosive growth occurs. You'll wake up one morning to see a field of daisies abloom in your heart. You'll inwardly feel God's love, personal and vibrant, directed toward you. And your heart will reciprocate almost effortlessly. These are precious moments to treasure.

However, most of the growth that makes those explosive seasons possible will take place during those times of life that seem mundane to us. Wake up, go to work, come home, go to bed. Over and over again. Did the seed take? You'll be tempted to respond like Mr. Toad by putting your head close to the ground and loudly saying, "Now, seeds, start growing!"

Perhaps you work yourself into exhaustion, practicing whatever spiritual exercise you can find to create growth: reading your Bible, going to church services, maybe even attending a conference or seminar. Like Toad, you may find yourself collapsing in exhaustion, despairing whether anything is occurring. "Is it even worth all this effort?"

Outwardly to others, perhaps even from your own scrutinizing gaze, nothing is happening. The soil of your heart will seem dead and unproductive, but growth is occurring! Roots are expanding and forcing their way down into the soil. Activity is happening under the surface. You are being rooted and grounded in such a way that long-term growth will be possible. Love is being stitched together inside. This love is something that will weather the storms of life.

For this reason, the Apostle Paul prayed:

> ...that according to the riches of his glory he may grant you to be strengthened with power through his Spirit in your inner being, so that Christ may dwell in your hearts through

faith — that you, being rooted and grounded in love, may have strength to comprehend with all the saints what is the breadth and length and height and depth and to know the love of Christ that surpasses knowledge, that you may be filled with all the fullness of God. (Ephesians 3:16-19 ESV)

The foundation of a healthy and sustainable Christian life is built inwardly. It requires being "rooted and grounded" in God's love. It requires forming connections with the Father, just as a seedling sends out roots to give it a secure foundation. It's hidden growth that comes as the relationship is nurtured.

> **THE HEIGHT OF A SKYSCRAPER IS LIMITED, NOT BY THE SKY OVERHEAD, BUT BY THE STRENGTH OF ITS FOUNDATION. THE FOUNDATION MUST BE FIRMLY SET BEFORE THE VISIBLE GROWTH CAN TAKE PLACE.**

Before you turn outward, you must turn inward. The height of a skyscraper is limited, not by the sky overhead, but by the strength of its foundation. The foundation must be firmly set before the visible growth can take place.

Learning to Trust

In 2014, my wife and I made a decision that would forever change our lives. We adopted a five-year-old boy. Adoption had been something we had talked about before, but it was always set aside for the future. We already had three biological children of our own, all boys, and we planned to one day adopt a little girl— or so we thought. When someone approached us about the opportunity to give this little boy a "forever home," I was caught entirely off guard.

My wife went through her "prayer and listening" phase quickly. Had I not known her, I would have presumed she skipped it altogether. In this situation, she apparently had a direct line to heaven. She was the first to be on board with the idea. The responsibility now shifted to me.

It took me much longer to figure things out. I spent several weeks praying, all the while, hoping that God would provide an obvious answer. "Lord, could it please be spoken audibly or through some other unmistakable way?"

I'm sorry to disappoint you, but he didn't answer that way. In fact, I find that *most* of the time, that's not how he speaks to me.

It would have been easier to hear a simple yes or no. "Thanks for the answer, Jesus. I'll be off on my merry little way." Instead, God gave me a choice. Now, it's one thing for my wife to put the responsibility on me. It's something entirely different when God is the one asking the questions. Instead of an answer, *he* asked me a question. Here I was, just living my life, going about my day. I was doing nothing remotely "spiritual" when I heard him speak within my heart and ask, "Will you do this for me?"

God gave me a choice. There was no one else on which to rely. It was entirely up to me. I could choose either option. Talk about feeling the pressure! At that moment, I felt as if I were standing on a cliff, contemplating a jump into the ocean below. He again asked, "Will you do this *for me?*"

I felt suspended at that moment in time. *What if I make a mistake?* I thought. Then, gently, without me even asking, I felt the peace of God fill my heart. There was a confidence that filled my heart, right alongside the uncertainty with which I was wrestling. Though I didn't have the words in the moment to describe it, God was extending to me an invitation. And it was up to me to respond. I said, "Yes," and jumped.

It's a different experience to adopt an older child. When you have a newborn, everything is fresh and new. They are a clean slate. When this precious boy joined our family, however, we quickly realized he carried with him some significant emotional trauma. The honeymoon phase, if we had one, was gone in a moment. Together with our son, we were thrown into a crucible.

He was filled with anger, hurt, and confusion. By the time he joined our family, he had spent more time in the foster system than with his biological parents. I can't imagine what he endured. A five-year-old brain is simply not prepared to handle a harsh world filled with drug abuse, neglect, and grief — quite honestly, no one is equipped for that.

Let's take a step back for a moment. In general, the cry of a baby produces some discomfort. Have you ever tried to keep sleeping when a baby wakes up upset in the middle of the night? Good luck with that! Whether the child is hungry or needs attention, a concerned parent will soon respond. This type of trigger and response has been engineered by God. The call of a baby produces results. This cycle gets naturally repeated 100,000 times over the first year of a baby's life.

Researchers have noticed something very significant occurs during this process. The baby comes to realize that his cry will produce a healthy response — a diaper change, a feeding, funny adult human faces at which to giggle. The cry-response cycle creates a bond between the infant and his parents. This all occurs naturally and by design.

In the process of adopting our son, however, we realized that not enough of his infant cries had been met with a healthy response. He didn't know whether his needs would be met. Imagine being a young child and feeling as if you had to care for yourself. Imagine feeling like no help would come. It was heartbreaking.

We didn't know half of what we were committing to when we adopted him. Even so, we were entirely committed to him. Zach would be treated just like our other boys. We would love him and provide for his needs no matter what the cost. Just like God treats us, we also would have no second-rate sons.

In those early stages, we did our best to prove ourselves trustworthy, but Zach didn't trust us. He had lived in a world of disappointment and broken promises for far too long. Manipulation was a coping mechanism that Zach had learned to use to survive. Even though he was in our home and had access to all our resources, he hadn't learned to rely on us to meet his needs.

There was a song I often heard when I was a teenager, by the band DC Talk, called "Luv Is a Verb." That could have been our theme song during those first months. We began demonstrating our love for him in a very tangible way. Whenever he expressed a need, my wife or I would provide a healthy response. This cry-response cycle was repeated over and over again. Due to his trauma and learned behavior, most of our "loving" was rejected. We were fighting what felt like an uphill battle, but God gave us the strength to persist. There's a verse in the Bible of which I was often reminded: "Love endures long and is patient and kind…" (1 Corinthians 13:4 AMP). We "endured long" for our little boy, not because we are particularly brilliant people, but because we had this simple goal: to love him.

We learned a lot about parenting during that season. God also used many scenarios with our adopted son to teach us about himself. It shouldn't have surprised me, but it did. I never expected to learn who God was by loving someone else. The best kind of lesson is the one acquired through experience.

One of the most common ways God describes himself to us is as a father. In the parable of the Prodigal Son, he's the one who was scanning the horizon, waiting for his rebellious son to come home. On the day he saw his son walking down the road, headed back in shame, he *ran* to meet him and embrace him (Luke 15). Is that shocking to you? God is so much better than we think.

When we respond to God's invitation, he adopts us into his own family (Ephesians 1:5). Having been adopted into his family, I bring *a lot* of baggage from my past. Even though Father God is fully committed to me and willing to respond to my every cry, there is still a process for me to learn to rely upon him. I have to learn to trust him, even as my adopted son had to learn to trust me.

When we adopted our son, there was a legal decree that went into place. We have court documents that established us as his parents. He received a new birth certificate, which showed us as his birth parents. And as for his past? All records of his original birth certificate were eliminated. His history has been legally rewritten.

Yet, it wasn't enough to simply have a piece of paper that proved he belonged to our family. Zach's heart didn't recognize those papers. Though the legal problem has been solved, there was still the issue of bringing healing to this boy's heart. The documents gave us authority. They proved we had assumed responsibility and guardianship over him for the long haul. But it was only a first step. He still needed a heart connection with us.

Scripture says we are taken out of the kingdom of darkness and brought into God's family in a sudden motion (Colossians 1:13). It is definite. Old records are expunged, and a new identity is created. However, the truth still needs to be applied to my heart. I must learn to live *into* the truth. What is reality and accepted as fact by my mind must still travel the long eighteen-inch journey into my heart.

Just as Zach had to learn to trust his mom and me, we must come to believe that our cries to God won't fall on deaf ears. Father God is present and eager to meet our needs if only we'll let

> **JUST AS ZACH HAD TO LEARN TO TRUST HIS MOM AND ME, WE MUST COME TO BELIEVE THAT OUR CRIES TO GOD WON'T FALL ON DEAF EARS.**

him. This is the life Jesus modeled for us. This is the invitation that has been extended to all, to grow in trust and learn that the Father himself loves you dearly (John 16:27).

He Wants to Hear Your Cry

My wife and I were learning how to love during this season. Zach was learning how to trust. And what was caught between us was rejection. When we would respond to his cries, he wouldn't always be willing to accept our love. He would push back on us, emotionally and sometimes physically. To be sure, Zach was processing a lot and had his own obstacles to overcome. But for us, it was tremendously challenging to love in the face of rejection. Rejection tests the quality of your love.

God's love is described this way: "Love bears all things, believes all things, hopes all things, endures all things" (1 Corinthians 13:7 ESV).

My love is weak, but God's love is strong. Can you believe God doesn't have a "hard time" with us? He doesn't grow tired. No matter how many times his love is rejected, his heart still remains open. And he keeps coming back! His emotions are strong and steady. There's always a fire hydrant of love and kindness directed toward you and me. Don't reject his love.

There is a verse in Psalms that says, "On the day I called, you answered me" (Psalm 138:3 ESV). There are two roles in this verse. There is the one who expresses the need and the one who answers. There is the one who calls and the one who responds. Can you guess which role you get to play?

God is not looking for self-sufficient people. He is looking for people who will call out, even cry out, to him. He wants to hear your voice, even if it sounds shrill or seems panicked or is angry. Prayer can be a very messy thing, and God is okay with that.

God's role is to respond. He wants to prove to you that he can be trusted. It is him communicating, "You are safe now. I know what you need." We need to unlearn the idea that God only wants strong and independent people. God doesn't operate within a budget, nor does he keep track of your cries as if there were a limit we must avoid reaching.

Father God is not looking for people to live extraordinary, epic lives. He's looking for the men and women who will invite him into the mundane, day-to-day, comings-and-goings of their lives. He is looking for people who will be honest about their needs, not to shame or belittle, but to prove in those moments the greatness of his love.

Will you open up your heart and allow him to respond to your cry? You're not responsible for the solution, only the cry. Learning to trust. Growing in love. These are lessons you never stop learning.

This can be frustrating for us "list makers" who enjoy the thrill of checking off boxes and sitting back, feet kicked up on the coffee table, and letting out one of those long sighs of satisfaction as we think, *Look at what I've done.*

I've been married to my wife for almost fifteen years. Even though we made a commitment back then, we still make a daily choice to love each other. It's something we nurture every day. There's never a point where we check it off our list and move on. The same applies to our relationship with God.

We are all on a journey as we learn to slow down, open up our hearts, and give ourselves permission to be loved deeply. I think Paul was touching on this when he wrote:

> Christ will make his home in your hearts as you trust in him. Your roots will grow down into God's love and keep you strong. And may you have the power to understand, as all God's people should, how wide, how long, how high, and how deep his love is. May you experience the love of Christ, though it is too great to understand fully. (Ephesians 3:17-19)

The process of learning how deeply you're loved by Father God is a never-ending journey. We were told, "for the Father himself loves you" (John 16:27 ESV). Still, we so easily take Jesus' words as a pleasant word of encouragement and not as the mind-blowing fact that it is God, who is by nature love, who has directed his attention toward us.

He doesn't possess love as a character trait; he embodies love itself. Whatever you've felt of love in your life has been but a glimmer, a cloudy reflection from the Source.

The invitation has been extended. Will you take a leap of faith and discover just how deeply you are loved?

Apply

Growth requires change. It's that simple. Throughout nature, we see the old adage proved true again and again: "If nothing changes, nothing changes." Every songbird has been pushed out of its nest. It's the only way its newly discovered wings can be put to use. All it takes is a little bit of courage and a nudge. The same is true for us. Through inward reflection, we discover our "wings," but it's only by application that we learn to fly.

Several suggestions for applying the truths from this chapter have been included below. This is not an exhaustive list. However, it should be enough to get you started. Find something that fits your personality. It should be action-oriented and push you just a little further than you feel comfortable.

- Gather five index cards. On each card, write down one truth about how God sees you or wants to interact with you. For example, "God wants to hear my voice, even if I'm having a bad day." You can use the material from this chapter if you need help with ideas. Place these cards somewhere you'll regularly see them - on the bathroom mirror, the dashboard of your car, or by your computer screen. Whenever you see the cards, read them aloud, and then pause to let those truths settle in your soul.

- Rearrange your morning routine to create space to connect with God. To create extra space, you could wake up a few minutes earlier or take a shower the night before. Sit down in a quiet place with your cup of coffee or tea and spend five minutes making yourself aware of his presence. If you don't feel anything initially, that's okay. When your mind wanders, just gently nudge it back with a simple prayer, such as "Father God, thank you for being here with me."

- Begin reading Scripture and looking for ways to connect with God through it. The Gospels (the books of Matthew, Mark, Luke, and John) are a great place to begin. Pray it back to him. When you read John 4:14, Jesus says, "But those who drink the water I give will never be thirsty again." Reply with your own prayer: "Jesus, I want to receive your water (i.e., his love) this morning."

- Take a few minutes to write down all the things you're good at and what brings you joy. Then ponder why God made you that way. Begin to think of it in terms of being created for a purpose and for connection with him.

_____

_____

_____

_____

_____

_____

_____

_____

_____

_____

_____

_____

_____

DO YOU KNOW JESUS?

Salvation is a lifelong journey, but you can enter this new life right now. If you have never made a choice to follow Jesus, I want to offer you that opportunity. Here is a simple prayer that can be used to respond to God's invitation.

"Jesus, I believe you are the Son of God and that you died on the cross to rescue me, both from sin and the spiritual death it brings. I'm in desperate need of you. I'm done trying to live life my way. I choose to turn away from my sin and my self-centeredness.

I'm saying yes to your invitation.

I receive your forgiveness and ask you to take your rightful place in my life as my savior and Lord. Transfer me from the kingdom of darkness into your family. Restore me, Jesus.

Now, come fill my heart. I welcome your love and your life. Live in me. Love through me. Thank you! Amen."

INDWELLING:
Living by the Power of God's Spirit

3

Trying to do the Lord's work in your own strength is the most confusing, exhausting, and tedious of all work. But when you are filled with the Holy Spirit, then the ministry of Jesus just flows out of you.
—CORRIE TEN BOOM

God will take upon himself the responsibility of making you full of the Spirit, not as a treasure which you must carry and keep, but as a power which is to carry and keep you.
—ANDREW MURRAY

I spent nearly every morning of my teenage life looking at myself in the mirror with disgust. Growing up overweight, I never had the physique of a model. You'd never find me wearing a Speedo to the swimming pool. Call it lousy genetics or just too much pizza and not enough exercise, the result was hard to accept. I'd curse my body in my thoughts and with my words.

In moments of despair, which were frequent, I'd turn to food and pornography to momentarily relieve the heaviness I carried. But the pleasure was short-lived. It quickly faded away, leaving me in my own prison of rejection and shame. In fact, I felt worse afterward than I did before.

One Sunday morning, I was standing in a church, singing with everyone else the old hymn "I Surrender All." After each chorus, the pastor would invite people to come forward to the altar, trying to elicit a response from the congregants who had been silently listening to him for the last hour.

"Are you ready to come forward to this altar?" he asked. "Will you take care of your business between you and the Lord?"

A few had already gone forward, and I knew he wouldn't wait much longer. My hands were firmly gripping the back of the pew in front of me, my heart was beating fast, and my mouth was bone dry. I knew I should go forward, but I couldn't help stalling a bit. I kept asking myself, *Do I really need to do this?*

Suddenly, I refused to delay any longer. I stepped out into the aisle and walked down to the altar in front of the church. I got down on my knees and tried to cry, because that's what you're supposed to do, right?

God, I give myself to you. I don't want to hold anything back. Despite the words I was praying, there was this nagging seed of doubt in my mind. I couldn't help asking, *Is it* actually *going to work this time? Will this spiritual experience* actually *take and produce a change in me? Will it deal with my addictions and self-hatred?* I felt conflicted inside but was desperate for something that would work.

This wasn't my first experience like this. I had responded to altar calls many times throughout my adolescence. But I couldn't ignore the fact that something was missing in my life. I was searching for a magic antidote to make my problems go away.

Each time, I would leave the altar wondering if I carried something new inside of me. Had some invisible deposit been made in my soul? Would it help me see myself differently or keep me from overeating or looking at porn on the computer?

My doubting thoughts would find validation. Not a week would go by, and I would fall back into the same bad habits. I was trapped in an endless cycle of defeat. In my heart, I wanted to please God and get it right. I felt as if I owed him that, at least. After what he had done for me, giving his son to die on a cross, how could I repay him with bad behavior and hopeless feelings of self-loathing? What a horrible way to live.

I felt inadequate to live this Christian life. No matter how I tried, I couldn't overcome the addictions that had their stranglehold on me. Like the Apostle Paul, I found that "I want to do what is good, but I don't. I don't want to do what is wrong, but I do it anyway" (Romans 7:19).

Having gone down to the altar all those times, I felt as if I should have stumbled upon the secret to get it right. All my years of study in Bible college hadn't uncovered the truth. Many years would pass until I discovered the key. But when it was finally revealed, I was forever changed.

But before we get to that part of the story, let's talk about running.

Having Gone Ahead of Us

In the book of Hebrews, we're encouraged to "run with perseverance the race marked out for us" (Hebrews 12:1 NIV). Truth be told, I hate running. In fact, I once almost bought a shirt that said, "If you see me running, you better run too because I'm being chased by something nasty." This verse is actually talking about a spiritual reality. Our life journey is compared to a long-distance race. Think of it as Spartan race with intimidating obstacles and plenty of dirt. No one is going to run a race like that without getting dirty.

But unlike most races in life, we don't know where we are headed or how long the journey will take. Despite all our dreaming and five-year and ten-year plans, all it takes is one small bump in the road to send us careening. Before we know it, we find ourselves in a place much different than we ever imagined possible.

We can have an idea of what lies ahead in life, but if we're honest with ourselves, we don't know the way nor how far the road will carry us. For that reason, it's comforting to know that the race has been "marked out for us." But who is it who has gone before us to prepare the way?

Consider the kindness of God. He has gone ahead and marked out a path for each of us to follow. He's inspected the way. He knows which direction we need to run and — if we get off course and stuck in the brambles of our own stubbornness or stupidity — he knows how to course-correct better than anyone else.

The race still lies ahead of us, so run to it we must. But we need not run it alone. It's for that reason we are encouraged to continue "fixing our eyes on Jesus" (Hebrews 12:2 NIV). Though he's already marked out the way for us, even now, he wants to run with us.

Do you see the kindness of the Father to give us such an example? The Father sent his Son, Jesus, who is himself fully God. Yet, in his coming to earth, he laid aside all his power and resources and took on our weakness. Jesus humbled himself and took on our human form (Philippians 2:8). He felt heartache, temptation, anger, and despair. He took ownership of our shortcomings so that he might become a perfect example for us to follow. Jesus ran the race as one of us — and won — so that we might confidently follow his example.

So how did he do it? How did Jesus live his life?

His Presence Changes Everything

Jesus believed in the nearness of the Father. To Jesus, the Father was not sitting on a cosmic throne far-removed from his situation. The Father was right there with him. Let's peer into this more deeply, because the insights we'll discover will become part of the answer for us.

While on earth, the question running through Jesus' mind was not, "How on earth am I going to run this race?" Instead, I believe his question was, "How are *we* going to do this?" Did you notice the subtle difference? The first question assumes he is alone, while the second question assumes they are a team.

Jesus was often in uncomfortable situations. He was followed by a group of self-righteous religious leaders almost everywhere he went. They listened to the words he spoke and the way he acted, looking for any opportunity to call out fault in what he was doing. Can you imagine how that must have felt? Being surrounded by constant criticism would be challenging.

In one such situation, Jesus said, "He who sent me is with me. He has not left me alone" (John 8:29 ESV). The Father didn't remain far away in the heavens. Instead, he accompanied his son. "I'm going to send you, son, but I'll be with you every step of the way." It was all about partnership.

This makes me think how, as a child, I used to get uncomfortable in large social environments. My family attended a church in Southern California that had several thousand members. It wasn't uncommon for several hundred people to be milling around in the church lobby before the service. I remember walking through the crowds, battling the loud chorus of people's conversations. Only four feet tall, I would be dodging in and out of groups of people. My eyes would be searching for one person: my dad.

He was almost always talking to someone, cracking a joke, a smile lifting the corner of his mouth. Always likable, he was the kind of person everyone wanted to have as a friend. Amidst that sea of people, I was nervous, but he was at peace. In fact, he was in his element, laughing and carefree.

I would run up and grasp his large hand, made rough by years as a roofer. They were strong hands, capable of hauling bundles of shingles around a job site, but to me, they were tender. With my hand in his, my anxiety disappeared. His confidence became my confidence. I found myself listening to my father's conversation and laughing at his jokes. His presence and demeanor redefined the situation that I was in.

I believe the Father was present with Jesus in a very similar way. His carefree ease transformed every scenario into a place of rest. "He has not left me alone." Jesus was never abandoned. Jesus was always supported. Storms could be raging all around, but you'd still find him sleeping in the boat (Mark 4:38-40). The Father's presence changed everything.

The same holds true for you. Why? Because you are loved by Father God. Whether you're aware of it or not, his presence was by your bed when you woke this morning. His presence has followed you throughout your day. Don't think for one moment that just because you hopped in your car and drove all around town running errands, he couldn't keep up with you! Truth be told, he can do it even better than you can. Have you ever been aware of God's presence in this way?

Despite how much people claim to know about God, his power, and extravagant love, it's still possible to live like an orphan - alone. You can hold an open invitation for a relationship, to be connected to God and enjoy all the benefits of being in his family, and yet live functionally unaware of his nearness. Are you content with that? I'm not.

We must call the truth back to remembrance. We must once again apply the truth to our orphan-prone hearts. Join me in believing, "But as for me, how good it is to be near God!" (Psalm 73:28).

Worldly thinking says, "Be independent. Do it yourself. Don't ask for help." But for those who follow Jesus, dependence is a virtue. In fact, even Jesus freely admitted, "I can do nothing on my own" (John 5:30 ESV).

God welcomes the opportunity to partner with you throughout your day. He's not interested in a family full of Lone Rangers. You don't have to feel left alone, asking, "How on earth am I going to get through the day?" Many people run from God in weakness when, in fact, he wants us to run to him. You can turn to God and, like Jesus, ask, "How are *we* going to do this?"

Washing Dishes, Being a Branch

Jesus lived his life in partnership with the Father. He relied on him entirely. Jesus said, "The Father who dwells in me does his works. Believe me that I am in the Father and the Father is in me" (John 14:10-11 ESV). The Father worked his miracles through Jesus.

Just the other evening, my boys were working on the dinner dishes. We had several guests over that night, which meant more dishes had to be cleaned. They weren't getting far, and I saw them struggling. So I got up from the table and helped them out. "Micah, you grab a cloth to dry the glasses. Noah, you stand by your brother and get ready to put things away." They stood there and obeyed my orders, mostly. When they got distracted, I reminded them of their job. And my role? With soap and washcloth in hand, I plowed through the dirty dishes. What would have taken them over an hour, we finished together in ten minutes. And the best part? When we were done, they got all the credit. And I was happy for them!

I like to think Jesus and his Father worked together similarly. When Jesus healed the man born blind from birth in John 9, it was the Father accomplishing his desire through his son. When an adulterous woman was brought before Jesus—having been singled out and on the brink of being stoned by a self-righteous mob—it was the Father behind the words, "Neither do I condemn you; go, and from now on sin no more" (John 8:11 ESV). The Father brought the power, the impetus, behind the works, but it was through Jesus that the Father's works were expressed. He perfectly reflected the Father, who dwelled in him. That's one fantastic partnership. And it's a model for how we can live today.

Let me provide a note for clarity. When I use the terms "indwelling" or the Father "dwelling in" Jesus, I am not speaking of possession in Hollywood movie terms. It's not a violent and disturbing manifestation where a person loses control or recollection of what happened. It's quite the opposite. The type of indwelling we see is one where the Father's desires were expressed through Jesus' personality, language, and culture. It was a partnership. Jesus yielded His life to the leading of the Father. He learned to follow the inner promptings placed on his heart.

Think about a tree. How hard does a branch need to work? Even now, as I write this, from my window, I see the wind whipping through the trees. The branches sway back and forth, seemingly hanging on for dear life. The job of the tree branch is to remain connected to the trunk of the tree. Period.

The branch has no life-giving supply on its own. If you cut a branch off from the trunk, it will soon wither and die. But as long as it remains connected, the life within the tree trunk is expressed through the branch. This is seen in the spring as leaves burst forth and then later in the summer when flowers and fruit develop.

When God's presence dwells within, you have access to all of his resources. And unlike us, he has no budget. His resources are limitless. Our job is to abide, to remain connected to him, as he produces his "fruit" through us.

Just Give Up

Jesus, who fully understood the importance of his ministry on earth, knew success in life was not dependent on his own abilities. Instead, he was able to trust or "rest" in his Father's strength. It was the Father who was doing the work. To enter this way of living, we must embrace a new way of thinking. What we believe determines our actions.

My younger self believed God wanted moral perfection out of me at the expense of everything else. I was so wrong. I couldn't even make it through the day. It's incredible how something so seemingly simple can be so impossible to produce. I felt shame. Instead of running to God when I failed, I withdrew from him. I turned my focus inward and resolved to try harder. Yet with each new resolution, I became more aware of just how powerless I was.

Had I known then what I know now, perhaps I wouldn't have wasted so much time. What God really wanted from me was intimacy, connection, and partnership. Jesus once said, "Yes, I am the vine; you are the branches. Those who remain in me, and I in them, will produce much fruit. For apart from me, you can do nothing" (John 15:5). He was waiting for me to finally give up and stop trying to do it on my own.

When trimming a tree, the cut branches may be lush and green at first. However, you'll soon notice a transformation taking place. Within just a few hours, the leaves will have lost their color and begun to shrivel up. What was once alive has now been overtaken by dryness and defeat. The branches can't survive alone. They need the moisture and nutrients from the trunk and the deep, invisible roots underneath.

You can't do it on your own. You'll never gain a lasting breakthrough by trying harder. No self-help mindset will alter this truth. There is no magical set of affirmations to speak over yourself. You can't will your way into perfection. Just give up.

If your experience is at all like mine, this is what happens. Let's say you listen to a song on the radio or read some inspiring words — perhaps even from this book — that carry you for a few days. Then, in a moment of weakness, you lose sight of what's right and do what you don't want to do (Romans 7:15). In an angry outburst, you yell at your spouse. On the way home from work, you call a friend and gossip about a coworker. You know you shouldn't, but you do it anyway. It feels satisfying in the moment, but it leaves you with a sense of failure and an awareness of just how powerless you are to fix yourself.

You will forever be a branch. A branch has no hope for lasting survival outside of the trunk, which gives it life. You were designed for dependence, and every attempt to live contrary to your created purpose will result in failure. To respond to God's invitation means giving up being strong and capable in your own right. You will discover God's strength by recognizing your own weakness (2 Corinthians 12:10) and running to him for help. This principle is for Jesus followers, both new and old.

Opportunity through Weakness

I know people who are obsessed with productivity. They're always talking about the latest bestselling book explaining a newly discovered life hack, offering them the hope of being more efficient. It's like a game to them, finding ways to check off more items from their to-do lists. Okay, I'll admit it: *I* am one of these people.

A few months back, I was driving home from the gym, listening to a podcast on productivity. The speaker was going through his list of the most useful productivity tips for the year. I was thoughtfully listening and taking inventory of my own life. Suddenly, I sensed the Holy Spirit speak to my heart. And he spoke in a rather opinionated tone, "Matthew, you know I'm really not that interested in upgrading you to the point where you no longer need me." Those words resonated within; it was a loving rebuke mixed with undeniable truth, in a way uniquely his own.

He went on to say, "You were never designed to do it on your own. I gave you those areas of weakness to make your need for me blatantly obvious." This was a new concept. I had always viewed my weaknesses as blemishes to be removed by any means necessary. But with a few words, the Holy Spirit had completely changed my perspective.

God sees weakness as an opportunity. Instead of being repulsed by my imperfections, he looks at them as a potter looks at clay, and says, "Yes, I can work with that." He looks beyond the outer surface and sees the beauty hidden within. And he chooses to reveal this masterpiece using his loving hands and immeasurable strength.

As I drove home down the country road, I thought back to all the times I went forward to the altar as a young man. I knelt at the altar. I cried at the altar. And then I left with the resolve to work harder on my own.

But there was something I had missed. That altar at the front of the church, a polished wooden bench made for kneeling and prayer, was a symbol for something much older and unpolished. In the Hebrew language, the word "altar" means a place of slaughter or sacrifice.

The imagery is throughout the Old Testament. An animal would be led to the altar, bound firmly, and then killed. The altar was a place where life gave way to death, where limits were reached. It was the end of the line for that which was sacrificed.

The ancient symbolism in the altar is still valid for you and for me. Every failure is an opportunity to recognize you have once again reached the end of yourself. Your strength has given out. The standard could not be reached. And the only reasonable response is to "die" by giving up on your own campaign and running to God for help.

As you make room for the Holy Spirit in your life, you'll discover grace to partner with God and walk in the steps of Jesus. It is through that place of indwelling that the accomplishes his works through your life.

The Apostle Paul said it best when he said, "My old self has been crucified with Christ" (Galatians 2:20). Again, there is that imagery of death and the end of yourself. Only then can you move forward. "It is no longer I who live. But Christ lives in me," he went on to write.

As any good father would, God allows you to reach the point of your weakness so that you can learn, and hopefully use, that experience to grow. Until you embrace this vital truth, be prepared for failure and burnout. You'll never be able to run on the mountains until you endure the failure in the dark valley of despair. It's in a place of darkness and weakness that we can all the more clearly see the grace of God that is available to us. As he says, "My power works best in the weakness" (2 Corinthians 12:9).

To be first, you must be last. To be exalted, you must serve. To be strong, you must embrace weakness. The kingdom of God is an upside-down kingdom. The Apostle Paul understood this reality and wrote, "So now I am glad to boast about my weaknesses, so that the power of Christ can work through me" (2 Corinthians 12:9). Embracing your weakness creates an environment where God can step in and work powerfully through you.

Reflect

Setting aside time to reflect allows us to become more aware of our inner selves and what God may be showing us. It's like a shopping mall directory, searching for the "You are here" arrow. Reflection helps us to understand where we are and where we want to go.

Allow your heart and mind to think about and process what we covered thus far, paying attention to your inner feelings, questions, and even frustrations. During reflection, we create space for God to search our hearts and expose things that were previously hidden. This results in an authentic connection, both with God and ourselves.

- Think about the areas of your life in which you have repeatedly struggled and failed to overcome. There may be an area of insecurity, a hidden addiction, or a destructive lie you've chosen to believe. Take a minute or two to think about this struggle and how it has impacted your life.

_____

_____

_____

_____

_____

_____

_____

_____

_____

- Where are you in the fight? Have you lost hope and given up? Are you angry at yourself or God? Be honest with your emotions. Don't hold back. You might find it helpful to share directly with the Holy Spirit by praying, "Holy Spirit, I feel _____."

_____

_____

_____

_____

_____

_____

_____

_____

- Most of the time, our struggles persist because we try to fix our problems alone. "I'll just try harder," we say to ourselves. But the truth is that you can't do it on your own. As you feel led, use this as an opportunity to repent of this self-effort-centered thinking. Keep in mind that repentance is less about saying you're sorry and more about committing to change direction.

_____

_____

_____

_____

_____

_____

_____

_____

_____

- Lastly, ask the Holy Spirit to fill you with hope and help you see him as bigger than this struggle. Use the space below to write down any insight you receive during prayer.

_____

_____

_____

_____

_____

_____

_____

A Special Container

My father-in-law likes to occasionally stop by the house with a gallon tub of vanilla ice cream for the kids. My kids aren't used to eating many sweets, so it's always a highlight for them. Who knew five dollars could make such an impact. The kids quickly devour the ice cream, resulting in sugar-induced craziness, which gets them sent outside to burn off their energy.

While some may throw away the empty container, not us Berrys. What do we do with the ice cream pail when it's empty? It's too useful a container and too valuable to just toss. So for several years, we've made it our habit to use the ice cream pail as a container for compost.

One day, we went to a birthday party with my youngest son, who was probably four at the time. As we were waiting for the cake to be cut, he pulled on my shirt and whispered, "Dad…" The tone of his voice showed he was clearly confused and a bit unsettled. He pointed at the ice cream pail on the counter and said, "Look, they filled up their compost bucket with ice cream!"

My four-year-old had only ever known those plastic pails to hold food scraps. Were they really going to serve compost with cake? He never imagined they were designed to hold something else. The contents of a container can drastically change the way that we view the container itself.

The Apostle Paul wrote about how "in a large house, there are containers that are used for honorable purposes and dishonorable purposes" (2 Timothy 2:20 ESV). Some containers can hold sweet vanilla ice cream, and some containers can hold compost—the unpleasant kind that has been sitting underneath the kitchen sink for several days.

Paul continued: "If anyone cleanses himself from what is dishonorable, he will be a vessel for honorable use, set apart as holy, useful to the master of the house, ready for every good work" (2 Timothy 2:21 ESV). A bucket that has been filled with compost can be thoroughly washed with soap, run through the dishwasher, and once again used as it was initially designed. Fill it with ice cream, and it once again becomes an ice cream bucket. The contents transform the container.

THE CONTENTS TRANSFORM THE CONTAINER.

Here's the point: You were created to hold something. The real question is, what do you hold? Do you carry criticism, hopelessness, or irritation around with you? Or are you full of hope, joy, and love? What are you serving to those around you? The contents of your container matter.

King Solomon, at the dedication of the Temple in Jerusalem, a thousand years before Jesus was born, remarked, "But will God really live on earth? Why, even the highest heavens cannot contain you. How much less this Temple I have built!" (1 Kings 8:2 ESV). Solomon was wise to presume that God's greatness could never fit in a building made with human hands.

Yet something marvelous happens when you commit yourself to follow Jesus. You become a new creation (2 Corinthians 5:17), capable of housing God's very presence. You become a container designed by God, not to hold everyday things like ice cream or compost, but to hold his very presence. God made it possible for his Spirit to dwell in you.

The Apostle Paul asked the early believers, "Do you not know that you are God's temple and that God's Spirit dwells within you?" (1 Corinthians 3:16 ESV). He wanted to make sure they didn't overlook this marvelous reality. It's a paradox that God's presence, though too immense to be contained by the highest heavens, can somehow dwell inside you.

You were created to carry the very presence of God, to be his vessel, the place he calls home. Your brain will try to rationalize this concept, thinking, "Sure, I get a small piece of him." But it's not so. God does not divvy out a sample-sized portion of himself to each of his children. You get *all* of him. Each of us gets all of him.

As A.W. Tozer so eloquently put it: "An infinite God can give all of himself to each of his children. He does not distribute Himself that each may have a part, but to each one, he gives all of Himself **_as fully as if there were no others_**"[3] (emphasis mine).

If you're not familiar with the Holy Spirit, there are a few important things to know about him. Just as with any person, it'd be impossible to describe him using a list of bullet points. However, this should serve as a good "crash course" to set a context for what will follow in this chapter.

The Holy Spirit is a person, not an impersonal force. He has thoughts, emotions, and a will to make decisions. (1 Corinthians 2:10, Romans 15:30, Ephesians 4:30, 1 Corinthians 12:11, 2 Corinthians 13:14)

The Holy Spirit is equally God, alongside the Father and Jesus the Son. We refer to this mystery as "the Trinity." They are equally divine. All have existed since eternity past. All are the same God, three persons in one. (Matthew 28:18-20, Acts 5:3-4, Ephesians 4:30)

The Holy Spirit teaches, reminds, and still speaks to us today. He is a very active participant in our daily lives and comes alongside us to help us follow Jesus. (John 14:26, Acts 8:29, Acts 13:2, Romans 8:26-27, 1 Corinthians 2:13)

The Holy Spirit does not operate on his own. He is always in complete agreement with the Father and Jesus the Son. He delights in taking what belongs to Jesus and sharing it with us. (John 15:26, John 16:14, 1 Corinthians 2:10-11)

His Fruit in You. His Fruit for You.

For several years, one of my boys struggled with fear at bedtime. He would come downstairs to our room terrified, at least once or twice a night. There were many times I felt frustrated and didn't know what to do. I would try to reason with him. Even though there were no intruders in our home, the feeling of fear still remained very real to him.

My son explained how he would wake up in the middle of the night with a tangible feeling of fear. It seemed to him as if every prayer was being catapulted far away into the heavens, and the answers he sought were out of reach. In those moments, he felt alone and vulnerable.

One day, I took him out for the afternoon. While we were driving, I whispered under my breath, "Holy Spirit, will you help me? Show me how to help my son overcome fear." I was desperate for a solution.

At that moment, I felt the Holy Spirit speak to my heart. He showed me a picture of my son. My son had this empty space in his chest, which was then filled with a miniature apple tree. The tree was full of red apples, beautiful and ready to be picked. There was so much fruit on the branches that they were nearly touching the ground.

The Holy Spirit reminded me of how he takes up residence within us when we turn from our sins and respond to his invitation. From that point forward, he dwells inside and begins to produce his fruit. Everything we could ever need comes from within, but it comes from him. It's not your fruit; it's his fruit.

What kind of fruit does the Holy Spirit produce? Scripture is clear about this. "The fruit of the Spirit is love, joy, peace, patience, kindness, goodness, faithfulness, gentleness, and self-control" (Galatians 5:22-23).

God heard my fatherly cry and answered me. I stopped the car, turned to my struggling son, and shared how his remedy was not far off. In fact, it was already within him. The Holy Spirit was actively producing the joy and the peace he needed during those fearful episodes. It was there for the taking if he would choose to believe. He could draw strength from God who dwelled within, rather than allow fear to tackle him. That revelation was a turning point in his battle with fear.

We need to give up trying to produce fruit on our own. "I'll just try harder," we insist. But we all know where that leads: exhaustion and empty hands. I can no more produce the Holy Spirit's fruit in my life than dirt can produce an apple. Our job is to host him well so that he, by his limitless resources, can produce the fruit in our lives we so desperately need.

It is possible to live above your struggles. To do this, you must first recognize the presence of the Holy Spirit within you in your time of weakness. Call out to him. He's not far away. He's closer than your very breath. Then you ask him to do the thing he so desperately wants to do in your life:

> **"PRODUCE IN ME WHAT I CANNOT PRODUCE IN MYSELF!"**

"Produce in me what I cannot produce in myself!"

The answer will not arrive in a FedEx box from the other side of the United States or far off in the heavens. The answer comes from within, from the place where the Holy Spirit dwells. Inside the "ice cream bucket" of your soul that houses the very presence of God, he produces his fruit.

The more time you spend with him, the more you will find yourself turning to him and allowing him to produce fruit in your life. The more you do this, the more you'll discover that the Holy Spirit is an expert at everything. From his unlimited resources, he will provide what you need. And it's a good thing — because only the Holy Spirit can live the Christian life.

"Those who say they live in God should live their lives as Jesus did" (1 John 2:6). If Jesus lived his life by the abiding presence of the Holy Spirit, who empowered him to do the things that the Father wanted to do, then so can you.

He's Waiting for Your "Yes"

So how do you receive the Holy Spirit? What does that even mean? It's a straightforward question, but there are probably as many opinions as there are chocolate chip cookie recipes on the internet. So I'm going to do my best to make this simple. I'm a firm believer that the good news of the gospel should be something even a child can comprehend.

The most straightforward explanation I've found comes from Acts chapter two. Peter is speaking to a crowd in Jerusalem on the day of Pentecost. On that day, the Holy Spirit was poured out, which marked a significant shift in human history. The Spirit came down and filled the room where the disciples were praying. And he, the Holy Spirit, rested upon each of them with a visible sign of a flame of fire.

There was a thundering noise that drew the visitors in Jerusalem to a central place, and Peter, filled with the Holy Spirit, spoke. He declared Jesus had risen from death in victory, and the Holy Spirit had been made available to all. Peter told them, "Repent and be baptized, every one of you in the name of Jesus Christ for the forgiveness of your sins, and you will receive the gift of the Holy Spirit" (Acts 2:38 ESV).

The Holy Spirit is a gift. He is a gift given to you. And like all gifts, it's not something that can be earned. You receive the Holy Spirit just as you receive salvation: by voicing a "yes" within your spirit. You simply accept him.

During elementary school, many years ago, kids would pass notes to one another. It was not uncommon for a young boy or young girl to rip off a square of notebook paper and, with their pencil, scribble the question, "Do you like me? Circle yes or no."

That little scrap of paper would be folded up and passed from student to student to the recipient. When the note was opened up and read, a choice had to be made. Do I like this person? Do I receive this gift of affection?

Receiving the Holy Spirit is just as simple. Circle yes or no. Do you want more of God's influence in your life? Are you willing to receive the gift he has for you? Because when that yes is voiced from within, no matter how small your yes might be, God honors that and fills you with his presence.

While on one of his missionary journeys, the Apostle Paul asked some believers in Ephesus, "Did you receive the Holy Spirit when you believed?" (Acts 19:2 ESV).

Interesting, isn't it, that he was looking for that distinction in their lives. Not, "Have you read any of the early Gospel accounts?" or, "Have you been sure to keep the Ten Commandments and live a godly life?" Could it be that he understood how vital the indwelling of the Holy Spirit was to a lifestyle of following Jesus? I believe so.

"Do you have the Holy Spirit?" Paul asks. And they said, "No, we have not even heard that there is a Holy Spirit" (Acts 19:2 ESV). When you are brought into the family of God, the Holy Spirit is made available to you, but he waits to be received. The Holy Spirit, God himself, waits for you to open up the door and let him in.[4]

Regular Refills, Greater Access

Throughout your life, you will repeatedly receive the Holy Spirit. Sometimes you'll feel it when you receive him. You may cry or tangibly sense the nearness of his presence. But at other times, all you will have is faith. All you will have is the belief that "I said yes and welcomed him in, so he's there."

Try not to think of receiving the Holy Spirit as a one-time transaction. Remember, he's not a thing to possess, he's a person to enjoy. Just as we talked about our relationship with God being a lifetime of growth and increased intimacy, the same is true for the indwelling Holy Spirit.

The Apostle Paul would later write to those believers in Ephesus and tell them to "be filled with the Holy Spirit" (Ephesians 5:18). The meaning in the original language is "be <u>continuously</u> filled with Holy Spirit." It's more than a single event. Instead, we spend every day welcoming his presence into our lives.

When the greatest evangelist of the nineteenth century, D. L. Moody, was asked why he said he needed to be filled continually

"I NEED A CONTINUAL INFILLING BECAUSE I LEAK!"

with the Holy Spirit, he replied, "Well, I need a continual infilling because I leak!"

Like Moody, we all reach a point where we need a fresh touch of the power of the Holy Spirit in our lives.

Over time I continue to open up my heart more and more to the influence of the Holy Spirit. Perhaps it's not only that I "leak," but that I am increasingly made aware of areas in my life that are closed off to him. These are places that I have not yet given him permission to occupy.

It's as if my life were a house. Inside my house, there are rooms and hallways and doors. The first time I invite a guest into my home, most of my doors are closed. My bedroom door is shut, hiding all the dirty clothes that are piled on my bed. My office, the dumping ground for all odds and ends in the house, is closed off so as not to embarrass me. But I find that as the guest continues to visit, as we get to know one another, my comfort level increases. I don't feel the urge to close all my doors when they visit. I allow them to enter the mess and see the real me.

"Since we are living by the Spirit, let us follow the Spirit's leading in every part of our lives" (Galatians 5:25). As we live in partnership with the Holy Spirit, we open up areas of our life to him and give him permission to influence those areas. The goal of this process (which is called "sanctification") is that eventually, he will have access to every room in my house. There is nothing hidden from him.

Face it. He's God, the all-knowing one. He already knows your dirty laundry is lying atop your bed behind that closed door. He's already aware of the mess in your office. A door isn't going to hide it from him.

As you learn to trust him and discover firsthand how kind he is and how gently he relates to us, you will find yourself more willing to open up those closed-off areas to him. As you open up to him, he will flood into that area of your life and begin to produce his fruit. The dirty laundry will get washed, folded, and put away. But to experience that kind of fruit, you must be willing to receive him and grant him access to those less-than-desirable places in your heart.

So what happened to that young man who was stuck in a cycle of constant failure? I wish I could tell you that there was a moment when the dark sky parted, and I received some life-changing revelation. Those moments can undoubtedly happen. I pray that happens to you as you read this book.

For me, however, my freedom was discovered slowly. Victories occurred along a path of regular failures. However, with each new revelation — about myself and my weakness and about God and his consistent presence — I found myself more open to the influence of the Holy Spirit.

It was as if the Holy Spirit, once invited into my "house," refused to leave. When each new "mess" was discovered, hidden behind barriers I had erected, he stayed around. He asked me, "Can I have access to that area of your life? It doesn't intimidate me. I love to clean up messes." His enthusiasm in the face of my brokenness showed me his kindness.

He proved kind, yes, but also committed for the long journey ahead. God doesn't run at the sight of sin in your life. He taught me how faithful he was, not through a class or podcast, but by getting his hands dirty, cleaning up the messes in the hidden areas of my heart. He showed me just how good he is at producing his fruit in those dark "compost piles."

The Holy Spirit produced his love in my heart first. That was the first crop. As I fed on that fruit, I began to love myself. I began to see myself through his eyes. My critical spirit no longer was the source from which I lived. When I saw myself in the mirror, I began to see the good and not the bad. If God loved me, I had permission to love myself.

> **IF GOD LOVED ME, I HAD PERMISSION TO LOVE MYSELF.**

The Holy Spirit then produced self-control in the fertile soil of his love. As I grew into this new perspective, I found myself being guided differently. I had a renewed desire to be with him and run toward him in times of weakness rather than away.

He proved his gentleness to me again and again. I came to realize that he's okay with my messiness, so long as I continue to extend him welcome and give him permission to express His life through me. He was never looking for perfection. He was looking for a companion.

Apply

Growth requires change. It's that simple. Throughout nature, we see the old adage proved true again and again: "If nothing changes, nothing changes." Every songbird has been pushed out of its nest. It's the only way its newly discovered wings can be put to use. All it takes is a little bit of courage and a nudge. The same is true for us. Through inward reflection, we discover our wings, but it's only by application that we learn to fly.

Several suggestions for applying the truths from this chapter have been included below. This is not an exhaustive list. However, it should be enough to get you started. Find something that fits your personality. It should be action-oriented and push you just a little further than you feel comfortable.

- Open your Bible and read Galatians 5:22-23. This passage describes the fruits that the Holy Spirit wants to produce in your life. Pick one that you'd like to see brought forth in your life. Go to the store and buy a small plant that can sit on your counter or in a highly trafficked place. Write the name of that "Holy Spirit fruit" on the pot. Use this as a visual reminder. Whenever you walk past, pray, "Holy Spirit, please produce your fruit in my life. I want to thank you for choosing to live your life through me."

- Find a quiet place during the day, perhaps during your lunch break. Turn on some instrumental music that will help you relax and slow down from the busyness of the day. Take a few slow, deep breaths in and then exhale. Think about how Jesus said, "Remain in me, and I will remain in you" (John 15:4). As you exhale, imagine releasing your concerns to God. Then, as you inhale, meditate on him coming inside to remain with you. Repeat this daily.

- Look at the picture of the tree below. Near the ground, write down some of the struggles that currently surround you. For example, "Uncertainty with work," or, "Conflict in the family." Then refer to the fruits that the Holy Spirit wants to produce in your life (Galatians 5:22-23). Write down all of the fruits you need to respond to your struggles. Draw them in or around the tree, just as if they were fruit.

Visit www.themattberry.com/tree-worksheet for a printable version of this image.

HAVE YOU RECEIVED THE HOLY SPIRIT?

Have you received the Holy Spirit, what the Bible sometimes calls the "baptism of the Holy Spirit" (Acts 1:5)? It's not hard to receive the Holy Spirit. There are only two things you must do. First, you must have accepted Jesus as your Lord and Savior and committed to a lifestyle of following him. You'll find a simple prayer to help you with that step in the Application section of Chapter Two.

The second step to receive the Holy Spirit is to ask him to come and fill you. The Apostle Paul, writing to the early church, asked, "Did you receive the Spirit by the works of the law, or by believing what you heard?" (Galatians 3:2). Receiving comes by believing. You don't need to do anything extra to capture his attention or convince him to come. The Holy Spirit is God's gift to you. Here is a simple prayer that can be used to receive the Holy Spirit.

"Father God, I'm here with you at this moment. I want to thank you for saving me through Jesus' sacrifice. Now, I pray that the Holy Spirit might come to me and fill me. This is your promise for me. I receive the Holy Spirit right now by faith, believing what you have promised. May your grace and the power of God come upon me and into my life right now. May I receive everything I need to follow you and live the life you want me to live. Thank you! Amen."

Now, having asked and received the Holy Spirit, spend a few minutes making yourself aware of his presence. Some people sense God working within them, whether in their spirit or through their emotions. Others don't feel anything. No matter how powerful or anticlimactic it may seem, write a quick thank-you in the space below. Thank him for giving you the presence of the Holy Spirit. Record the date and time so you can refer back to it in the future. Now, begin to live by the power of the Holy Spirit. Allow him to produce his fruit in your life!

PRAYER:
Seeing and Hearing What God is Doing

4

*What I've learned the more time I've spent following Jesus
is that God delights in answering our impossible prayers.*
—Bob Goff

The small prayers of weak and broken people move the heart of God.
—Mike Bickle

Is it possible to hear God's voice? If so, how can I do it? These are essential, relevant questions — foundational to life lived with God. Yet many Christians wrestle with the concept of connecting with God through prayer. It's actually quite ironic, especially since Christian belief has at its foundation a God who desires connection with us.

What are we left with if this relationship is missing? How can you trust in God without the experience of interacting with him and receiving from him? Wouldn't it seem unusual if I claimed to have a healthy relationship with my wife, but we never talked or experienced life together? From the outside looking in, you might think my marriage was in trouble and that I was just too ignorant to recognize it.

I realize it's a bit nebulous to say Christianity is based on a relationship. Let's make this idea more specific and concrete. A key component of following Jesus is our ability to hear his voice and respond to his particular words spoken to us regarding specific situations in life. Jesus said, "My sheep hear my voice, and I know them, and they follow me" (John 10:27 ESV). You can't underscore the importance of prayer in your relationship with Christ. As A.B. Simpson has famously said, "Prayer is the link that connects us with God."

Have you ever watched a shepherd leading his sheep? A shepherd doesn't position himself behind the sheep, driving them along like you would herd cattle. Instead, the shepherd goes ahead of the sheep. He calls out to them, even sings to them at times. By hearing his voice, the sheep know which direction they should walk. The same is true for us. We are designed to be led by the voice of God.

Several years ago, my parents regularly met with a small group of people from their church. They'd gather in one another's homes and talk about life and faith. With piping hot cups of coffee in hand, the group listened as the host began to share. "The pastor has been speaking about prayer lately. I'm curious, how many of you feel confident in hearing God's voice?" There was an awkward moment of silence.

One by one, the members of the group began to share their doubts and challenges concerning prayer. The group was filled with people from all walks of life: married people, single people, new parents, retirees, new believers, and people who grew up singing hymns and attending Sunday School. Despite their differences, all these people were sincere in their faith and committed to God, but they didn't understand how to hear his voice.

Only a handful of people had experienced prayer as a two-way dialogue. Two of those seasoned "listeners" were my parents. I'm proud of them. My dad, who dropped out of high school to put food on the table for his family, knows how to pray. My mom, who never taught a Sunday School class or went to Bible college, can recognize the voice of God. They learned to pray in the trenches of life. In the "nitty gritty," as my friend, Alan Ross likes to say. In their desperation, they chose to run toward God with their doubts, uncertainty, and frustration. They weren't always perfect at hearing his voice, but they kept coming back to him again and again.

Prayer challenges our belief that God exists. It's the defining factor that makes this Christian lifestyle more than just a code of ethics. Without encounters with God, we can't claim to interact with a divine being who is both personal and relatable. Francois Fenelon has famously said, "Of all the duties enjoyed by Christianity, none is more essential and yet more neglected than prayer." Prayer is the bridge that takes you from a place of knowing about God to a position of understanding him personally.

You can't read a book or watch a video to cultivate a life of prayer. It isn't an intellectual exercise. No amount of mental gymnastics can produce a life of prayer. That would be like watching the Tour de France on television and expecting it to teach you how to ride a bike. A life of prayer can only be developed by actually praying.

A LIFE OF PRAYER CAN ONLY BE DEVELOPED BY ACTUALLY PRAYING.

Your Voice Is Heard

Jesus modeled a life of prayer that was full of expression and that was infused with confidence. It was concentrated and pure and precious. It was everything our emaciated and faltering experiences are not. He lived his life with ongoing two-way communication with the Father.

To Jesus, prayer was not one-sided. He wasn't lobbing his requests out into the atmosphere, like sending spiritual postcards with no return address to the Father. He had confidence that his prayers were actually heard and that his Father would respond in kindness and speak directly to him.

This ability to receive wasn't a superpower granted especially to Jesus because he is God. In coming to earth, Jesus humbled himself and laid aside all the advantages he had as God. He took on our form and became one of us (Philippians 2:7-9). In his humanity, he deeply connected with Father God. The life of Jesus became the model we can use for ourselves.

Jesus had a dear friend named Lazarus who died unexpectedly. Jesus showed up to Lazarus' grave after he had already been buried. Mary and Martha, the sisters of Lazarus, approached Jesus with heart-wrenching sadness on their faces. They were in shock and filled with grief. It was an intensely emotional moment, causing even Jesus to weep.

Afterward, Jesus commanded the stone covering the tomb to be removed. Somewhat reluctantly, the men move the stone away. The pungent stench of death and doubt rush out of the crypt. But Jesus, who was aware of the Father's presence, lifted up his eyes to heaven and prayed.

"Father, I thank you that you have heard me. I knew that you always hear me. But I said this on account of the people standing around that they may believe that you sent me" (John 11:41-43 ESV).

And with that, Jesus cried out with a loud voice, "Lazarus, come out!" And the man who once was dead walked out of the grave, settling for all time that hope extends beyond the grave. Jesus had confidence that he was heard. He understood that his prayers didn't fall on deaf ears. His prayers reached beyond the unbelief of the crowd and into the very presence of the Father. The Father heard what he said.

Developing this kind of confidence doesn't happen overnight. Just like any relationship, it takes time to learn how to listen and understand what God is saying. However, what this story does give us is the confidence that God is always listening. So let's continue to dig in further and discover how to better hear God's voice for ourselves.

Shattering the Impossible

Jesus believed his voice was heard. He also knew that the Father spoke to him in reply. For Jesus, prayer was a two-way interaction. There was an exchange of thoughts and emotions. The Father spoke personally and directly to him. Prayer was the connection, and it formed the foundation for everything Jesus did. "Truly, truly, I say to you the Son can do nothing of his own accord but only what he sees the Father doing. For whatever the Father does that the Son does likewise for the Father loves the Son and shows him all that he himself is doing" (John 5:19-20 ESV). Prayer wasn't abstract or spooky to Jesus. He expected more than an empty monologue. He saw his Father engaged in this world and believed he was invited to join in the adventure.

The life of Jesus is laid out before us as a blueprint, shining a light on a path that we can follow. His experience can become our own. God hears your voice, and you can hear his. Nothing carries more potential to change your life.

Sadly, many people don't expect to hear from God in such a personal way. It'd be easy to look at the prayer life Jesus experienced and see it as something to be admired, but not experienced ourselves. But

I believe Jesus in his humanity modeled a doable lifestyle of prayer to prove that we can experience the same depth and quality of relationship with the Father.

Robert O'Neill once said, "Impossibilities only exist until somebody does it."[5] Jesus came to shatter impossibilities and to introduce a new normal. He removed every barrier and laid out a path for us to follow. Prayer can be personal, meaningful, and doable for ordinary people. The only limiting factor that remains is us. Will we believe it's possible?

In 1954, Sir Roger Bannister was the first man to run a mile in under four minutes. Until that point, it was believed the human body couldn't physically move that fast. Experts were convinced it would collapse under the pressure. As soon as he broke that barrier, though, people began to believe faster speeds were possible. Just forty-six days after Bannister broke the record, someone else beat his time. Once one man proved it was possible to run a mile in under four minutes, suddenly others were able to do it. Once you stop believing something is impossible, it becomes possible.

Don't define your theology, your understanding about God, or yourself by your own lack of experience. It's precisely for that reason that Jesus came to earth and lived among us. He showed us a different way of life. By following his example, we can experience the Father and connect with him through a lifestyle of prayer.

You Can Hear His Voice

If you have responded to God's invitation, what the Bible refers to as being "in Christ" (2 Corinthians 5:17), you can hear the Father's voice. It's available for you, completely independent of your own behavior, whether good or bad. It's that simple. You should expect to hear God's voice.

I want my children to hear my voice daily. Should they ever have something pressing to share, I try my best to keep these old ears open to them. In fact, there have been many times when I have been awoken from a deep sleep by the sound of one of my boys crying from two floors above my bedroom. Why would it be any different in our relationship with Father God? It reminds me of how Jesus once said, "So if you sinful people know how to give good gifts to your children, how much more will your heavenly Father give good gifts to those who ask him" (Matthew 7:11). If I'm an ordinary person and care about my kids this way, how much more does God care for you and me?

There are some Christians who believe God no longer speaks personally to us. They argue that since we already have the Bible, the only communication he needs to provide us is that which can be extracted from the page. The idea of receiving a personalized, direct word from God is viewed with disbelief. By the same logic, shouldn't it be enough for me to write a book to my children and then never speak to them again? Of course not!

> **I HAVE DISCOVERED THAT THE FATHER WILL BE AS TALKATIVE AND AS ENGAGED WITH YOU AS YOU CAN POSSIBLY HANDLE.**

I have discovered that the Father will be as talkative and as engaged with you as you can possibly handle. His thoughts for you can't be counted (Psalm 139:17). Imagine placing a glass bottle in a sink and turning on the faucet at full blast. Most of the water would flow over the sides of the container, not making it inside. Why? Because the bottle has a small opening. There's not a shortage of water; instead, there's a limit to what can be received. It's the same way with hearing God's voice. Though the Father's heart is overflowing with love, you and I will always be the limiting factor.

Although we may feel like a glass bottle with a small opening, we don't need to remain that way forever. God can change your glass bottle into a wide-mouth mason jar, capable of capturing more from him. You can learn to hear God's voice more consistently. And because God's love doesn't play favorites (Romans 2:11), you have just as much potential to hear him as anyone else. You're the only one who has your voice. The Father wants to hear it, and he wants to speak to you.

I think one of the greatest tragedies that can befall a Jesus follower is to look at others as being more favored or significant to God than ourselves. We can put them on a platform in our minds without realizing it. As a result, we can end up believing the lie that their experience can't be our own. We may even be tempted to think, "I'm *just* a stay-at-home parent," or, "I'm *just* a middle-aged worker bee stuck working a full-time job." We can feel unqualified or somehow at a disadvantage to hear God's voice.

I want to challenge you to dream big about what your prayer life could become. This requires faith. "Now faith is being sure of what we hope for, being convinced of what we do not see" (Hebrews 11:1 NET). Our entire Christian experience rises or falls on our faith. Think about how easily children will believe what they're told. They've not been bombarded by a lifetime of endless negativity and pessimism. They simply believe and allow their expectations to grow and their imaginations to run wild. Faith gives birth to hope and produces an expectancy of good things to come.

Come to Him at Your Worst

We are encouraged to confidently "draw near to the throne of grace that we may receive mercy and find grace to help in time of need" (Hebrews 4:16 ESV). Are you hungry for an encounter with God? You've been invited to draw near to him, not only when you are at your best, but particularly in your time of need.

If I received an invitation to have dinner with a famous person, let's say the Queen of England, you better believe I would wear my finest clothes. I would take a shower. I would shave. I would present myself at my best to her in order to show honor and respect. As queen, she'd expect it, even demand it.

But the picture that Scripture paints for us is quite the opposite. You've been invited to enter the presence of God even at your worst and in your brokenness. He's not frustrated with your weakness. He's not disappointed in your weak prayers. You'll not be placed in a time-out until you've behaved. In your failure, you are invited to approach him and hear his voice.

Last year, I did an interesting study. I read through the Gospel of John and looked for all the places where Jesus mentioned his Father. There are well over 100. The Father was with him. The Father knew him. The Father showed him things. In Jesus, we see one who is confident in his relationship with Father God. And it is out of that sense of identity that we see Jesus pray. He knew how loved he was. Do you?

In Scripture, we read, "He who did not spare his own Son but gave him up for us all, how will he not also with him graciously give us all things?" (Romans 8:32 ESV). The Father values you so much that he gave the most precious thing he had, his son, Jesus, to rescue you. He cancels your debt and calls you his friend. He gives you his Holy Spirit who dwells within you and will never leave. After all that, why would the Father withhold his voice from you? He won't.

Believe for a more significant experience with God than you've ever had before. Come with expectation. As you approach the Father in prayer, keep in mind that you are not heard because of the many words that you pray (Matthew 6:7). He hears every prayer, even those mumbled under your breath. In fact, he knows what you are going to say before the words come out of your mouth: "Even before a word is on my tongue, behold, oh Lord, you know it altogether" (Psalm 139:4 ESV). Father God's attention is always directed toward you. He hears your voice because you belong to him. There is no secret code you must learn.

A lifestyle of prayer is built upon the foundation of relationship. That's why we're addressing the topic of prayer at this point, because there is a build-up. You must first encounter God's love, because only then can you joyfully participate in the relationship. You were created for encounter; that's why he gives you the Holy Spirit to dwell inside you. He is near, and not far off. He is fully engaged and committed to doing life together with you. Hearing his voice is an extraordinary gift; we must daily respond to his invitation.

Reflect

Setting aside time to reflect allows us to become more aware of our inner selves and what God may be showing us. It's like a shopping mall directory, searching for the "You are here" arrow. Reflection helps us to understand where we are and where we want to go.

Allow your heart and mind to think about and process what we covered thus far, paying attention to your inner feelings, questions, and even frustrations. During reflection, we create space for God to search our hearts and expose things that were previously hidden. This results in an authentic connection, both with God and ourselves.

- Think about how you have approached God through prayer in the past. Has it been mostly during a time of crisis? When you have prayed, have you felt confident or insecure? Be honest with yourself. Take a few minutes to jot down some key phrases or ideas that summarize your experience.

_____

_____

_____

_____

_____

_____

_____

- God is continuously speaking to us, but we often miss his words because our "opening" to hear from him is small, like the glass bottle described in this chapter. Sometimes we carry limiting beliefs about ourselves or God, such as, "I'm too messed up," or, "God isn't interested in me." Use the space below to write down any thoughts that have made you feel unqualified to hear God's voice.

_____

_____

_____

_____

_____

_____

_____

- As we grow in prayer, we grow in faith. They are two muscles that get conditioned at the same time. Faith chooses to believe even if the emotions aren't there to support it. So while you may not feel confident hearing God's voice (see question 1), know that you still can. And while you may feel unqualified to hear God (see question 2), he again invites you to approach him. Use the space below to write a faith-filled prayer to God. For example, "I may feel insecure and not good enough, but I am choosing to believe you want to speak to me."

_____

_____

_____

_____

_____

_____

_____

- You were designed to hear God's voice in a personal and direct way. As you grow in this lifestyle of being connected to him, what are some things you'd like to discuss? You might find it helpful to express this as a written prayer in the space below.

_____

_____

_____

_____

_____

_____

_____

_____

Kitchen Experiments

As a younger man, I had hoped to find a guide or a step-by-step process that would make a lifestyle of prayer doable. While I never did find it, it's my desire that this resource could become that guide for you. Every person adopted into God's family is given the ability to hear his voice. That includes children, the uneducated, those who are exhausted by life, and even the mentally disabled. If you needed a Ph.D. to competently hear his voice, then most of us are in some serious trouble.

So let's demystify hearing God's voice. The truth is you've likely heard it before, but you didn't realize it.

Have you ever been driving down the road, and as you're zoning out, the image of a person's face comes into your mind? It may have been a friend you haven't spoken to in a long time. It may be that person you met in the grocery store a few months ago. Have you ever begun praying for that person as you're driving down the road? If so, then you've likely already heard God's voice and felt his nudge upon your life.

Have you ever faced a decision where you weren't sure which option to pick? As you pondered the decision, you got a strong sense that you need to choose option A rather than option B. It might not have made logical sense, but you knew that it was the right choice. If you've experienced this, you may have already sensed the Holy Spirit speaking to your heart.

Although most Jesus followers have felt God speak to them, it can be easy for us to doubt we have really heard from him. We explain it away as intuition or a gut feeling. If we were honest with ourselves, we would admit to wanting to hear from God more substantially, like a booming voice from heaven or a message from the clouds. Our hit-or-miss experiences can feel more like misses than hits.

I have some family members who like to experiment in the kitchen. They're much more adventurous than I am. To them, recipes are more suggestions than a set of instructions. Do you have any family members like that? While they've produced some delicious, never-before-seen desserts, at other times, they don't quite deliver what I'd consider delightful treats.

For many of us, our experience in prayer is like a cooking experiment. When we really hit on something, we feel confident it's coming from God. But most of the time, we feel like we're fumbling around with the wrong kind of measuring spoons and only half a recipe.

In the next section, I'm going to explain a method I've found particularly helpful to hear God's voice. But first, I'm going to show you a few examples of what my kids have recently heard from God. I'm sharing this with their permission. We as a family want you to see what the end product can look like and how beautifully and personally God can speak, even to children.

These examples should also help frame a response to the common question, "What should I expect God to say to me?" God's voice can be expressed simply, as in the form of a picture. It can carry a message poetically and with flowery language. There have even been times when I've written down three words and then illuminated them with a yellow highlighter because I knew they carried his mark.

As you listen for God's voice, expect it to be highly personal and relatable. He likes to use our own language. For that reason, how God speaks to me will likely be a bit different than how he speaks to you. Take comfort in that fact.

> **AS YOU LISTEN FOR GOD'S VOICE, EXPECT IT TO BE HIGHLY PERSONAL AND RELATABLE. HE LIKES TO USE OUR OWN LANGUAGE.**

Fall Into My Hands

—Micah, Age 6

Jesus says, "Micah, you can stop. If you fall, you'll just fall into my hands."

Seeing Jesus

–Noah, Age 7

I see Jesus. He's in a forest. He looks like emerald. He's touching me and I look like emerald too. What does that mean? Jesus says, "It means that you never have to feel like you're different from me, because you can have the same power as me. You're really growing in truth. I love you."

Surfing

–Judah, Age 11

> Judah B.   July 28 2016
> Me and Jesus are surfing on beach waves. Jesus tells me, "These waves are like my love. You will be able to let them carry you with them effortlessly. It is good to be in the presence of my love. Keep going with the wave of life. Do not try to surf in other places. there are dangers there. Just stay safely and happily on my love

Me and Jesus are surfing on beach waves. Jesus tells me, "These waves are like my love. You will be able to let them carry you with them effortlessness. It is good to be in the presence of my love. Keep going with the wave of life. Do not try to surf in other places. There are dangers there. Just stay safely and happily on my love."

Becoming Aware of His Presence

I'm going to share a simple and repeatable process to hear God's voice. However, I ought to post a disclaimer that this is just one way to connect with God in prayer. Many methods exist, and you ought to eventually try them all. But you have to start somewhere. This is an excellent place to begin if you're just getting started.

Let me give you one more piece of advice. While many methods can be used to pray, you'll eventually need to invest time in the "secret place" (Matthew 6:6) with God himself. No amount of study or discussion about prayer will, by itself, help you pray. There is no substitute. The person who would learn to connect with God must give themselves to a lifestyle of prayer.

The first step toward this deeper life with God begins with intentionality. Invite God into your day. Value his presence and welcome him, even verbally, to join you as you go to work or run errands.

Brother Lawrence was a monk who served in a Carmelite monastery in Paris in the 1600s. He is remembered for the close friendship he had with God. He once said, "I cannot imagine how religious persons can live satisfied without the practice of the presence of God." He went on to write, "We should establish ourselves in a sense of God's presence by continually conversing with him."[6]

A simple way to center your life on Jesus and to develop an awareness of his presence is to turn the activities of your day into prayers themselves. For example, as I look out the window during winter and see the bare trees, I'm aware that though the leaves have died and fallen off the branches, life is still flowing inside them. I'll pray to Father God, "Just as there may be winter in my soul, I know that spring will come."

I may be washing dishes in the evening. As the wet, soapy cloth pushes food off a dirty plate, I'll pray, "Father, would you cleanse my heart of any gunk that shouldn't be there?" I'll follow that prayer by listing some areas of anxiety and repenting for having yelled at my kids in a moment of frustration. Just as the food disappears down the drain, I thank God for his wholehearted forgiveness for me.

I may be mowing the lawn on a warm summer day. The bright sun is beating down, and I'll pray, "Father, would your love warm the cold areas of my heart?" Every mundane activity can become a launchpad for prayer.

> **AS THE WET, SOAPY CLOTH PUSHES FOOD OFF A DIRTY PLATE, I'LL PRAY, "FATHER, WOULD YOU CLEANSE MY HEART OF ANY GUNK THAT SHOULDN'T BE THERE?"**

Inviting God into your day can make even the most tedious and unbearable chores meaningful. What you're doing in these moments is making yourself aware of his presence and practicing keeping that two-way communication open.

God's presence is near, not far off. Paul said, "In him we live and move and have our being" (Acts 17:28 ESV). Just like spending an afternoon in the pool, he surrounds you like water. There's nothing needed to conjure his attention. By faith, believe he is near, and then jump right in!

Another way to invite him into your day is to mention his name. I have a habit of sighing at random moments throughout the day. I find that whenever I sigh, I breathe deeply and exhale. Often, I'll say his name repeatedly, "Jesus, Jesus, Jesus, Jesus, Jesus." I allow my breath to escape, and then I'll breathe in again and repeat his name again. Now, of course, it's not as if I'm calling him to come from far away. It's also not some magical incantation or mantra. I'm using his name to remind myself of his immediate presence.

You may find it helpful to set aside a few moments throughout the day to turn your thoughts towards God. Close your eyes and say his name or thank him for being with you. I've used set alarms on my phone to remind me; otherwise, I can get too caught up in my day. Remember: The most important thing is not the words you say, it's the heart behind it that longs for connection.

This will help you rewire your brain to be God-focused. When you do something long enough, you can turn it into a habit. By doing this, you are developing well-traveled neural pathways in your brain, so it will take less time to connect from one point to another. To accomplish this, you must be intentional at first. It will require some intentionality, but you can train yourself to be more aware of his presence.

Slow Down. Be Still.

The second thing you can do is set aside time to be still in his presence. Psalm 46:10 says, "Be still and know that I am God."

In Western culture, we tend to be driven and task oriented. Our lives are very different from the agrarian society in which Jesus lived. From the moment I wake up until I lay my head on my pillow at night, I can find myself running around frantically from one thing to the next. Making breakfast for the kids. Getting to work. Working through a backlog of email. Eating lunch in front of my keyboard because there is no time to spare. Having dinner with the family. Putting the kids to bed. Repairing the broken cabinet door. And then finally collapsing on the bed.

To develop a life of prayer, you actually have to pray. You actually have to set aside time to be still in his presence.

We've bought walkie-talkies for our boys on several occasions. Our kids get into a habit of trying to talk to one another at the same time. If you know anything about walkie-talkies, you know that if you hold the top button down, it opens the channel. The person on the other end can't say anything in response until you first let go of the talk button.

> **TO DEVELOP A LIFE OF PRAYER, YOU ACTUALLY HAVE TO PRAY. YOU ACTUALLY HAVE TO SET ASIDE TIME TO BE STILL IN HIS PRESENCE.**

The same is true for prayer. If you're running frantically through your day and not hearing anything from God, maybe you need to slow down and tune in to the right channel. And once you slow down, try not to talk the entire time. If you're always speaking to him, you're not likely to hear anything in response. Get your finger off the talk button. You'll find that as you stop, take a few deep breaths, and become comfortable with the silence, his presence will become easier to recognize. Slow down your body. Limit your words (Ecclesiastes 5:2). Let God speak to your heart in the silence.

As believers, we don't navigate our lives only by feeling. As it says in 2 Corinthians 5:7, "We live by believing and not by seeing." But we should recognize that our feelings were given to us by God. You were made to "love the Lord your God with all your heart, all your soul, all your strength, and all your mind" (Luke 10:27). This includes your ability to sense his presence. The Holy Spirit dwells within you.

My Thoughts or His Thoughts?

As you set aside time to be still in his presence, the Holy Spirit will begin to speak to you. I think it's best to set our expectations based on what Scripture says. In John 7:38, Jesus, speaking of the Holy Spirit, said, "Anyone who believes in me may come and drink! For the Scriptures declare, 'Rivers of living water will flow from his heart.'"

When the Holy Spirit dwells in you, living waters ought to flow out of you. That flowing doesn't come from your own intellect or your own emotional place; rather, the flow comes from the Holy Spirit himself. The way that it manifests in you is as a still, small voice. It's not something audible, but it is a voice that can be heard from within.

The best way to describe this flow is to compare the difference between the way my own thoughts are formed within me and the way the Holy Spirit's thoughts are formed within me. When I'm solving a problem, it feels as though the solution is built "brick by brick" inside my mind. For instance, I'll be thinking about a problem with the shed outback. I will begin by thinking, "Okay, number one: These are the tools that I need to fix it. Number two: I'm going to need to grab some wood from the garage. Number three: I'm going to need this type of screw." And so forth. The answer doesn't come to me immediately. It's something that I piece together.

In contrast, when the Holy Spirit speaks to me, it's as if fully completed thoughts are dropped into my mind. So at one moment, the thought was not there, and there was no building process occurring. At the next moment, a complete thought drops into my mind. It just "flows" from within.

It's almost as if somebody had walked into the room and shared their thoughts with me. For example, when my wife walks into the room and shares a thought with me, I have no part to play in the building of that thought. Her words are just presented to me, and I hear them. I find it's the same way when the Holy Spirit speaks. Even though I do not audibly hear his voice, there is that flow of living water — his complete thought presented in my mind. I like the way Dr. Mark Virkler describes this process in his book *4 Keys to Hearing God's Voice*, where he describes it as thoughts that "bubble up" from within.[7]

As you are spending time in the Lord's presence, as you become aware of his nearness, you're going to tune into those thoughts that bubble up. I find it helpful to ask a question of the Lord and then be quiet. The question helps provide focus to your interaction with him.

I strongly suggest that as you are beginning to hear God's voice within, that you not ask life-altering questions at first. For example: "Is this person going to be my wife?" Or, "Should I move to a different state?" Start small. You *will* make mistakes. It's better to fall off a bike during a leisurely ride around the park than to fall down a mountain bike course.

If you're just beginning, I challenge you to ask questions that are less directive and that have more to do with your identity. A great question to ask is, "God, what do you see when you look at me?" You can also ask, "What do you think about me?"

In 1 Corinthians 6:17, Paul writes that "the person who is joined to the Lord is one spirit with him." This is an amazing concept. When the Holy Spirit takes up residence within you, he actually joins himself to your spirit. This means there is no distinguishing between the thoughts that bubble up from your spirit or the Holy Spirit. You are one with him.

Visions and Your Imagination

As you tune in to the things God begins to show you, you may discover he speaks into your thoughts or even shows you a vision in your mind's eye. They are both equally valid. Seeing visions is not something we expect nor honor in our Western culture. In fact, it can make us feel downright uncomfortable. But in reality, we all see visions regularly.

For example, let's say I have a disagreement with somebody. I yelled at them and said something unkind. The only right thing to do is to call that person and apologize. If I'm feeling especially nervous, that upcoming conversation will play repeatedly in my mind. I'll find myself visualizing ways to avoid undue conflict. I haven't even called the person, and yet I feel as if I've already talked to them multiple times. I've anticipated the different results by saying this or that. This is a kind of self-directed vision, and it happens more than we notice.

Our minds are incredibly active. This type of anxiety-driven vision doesn't come from the Holy Spirit; it comes from our unsettled emotions. The truth is that we are much more familiar with imagination and vision than we give ourselves credit. Our imagination is a tool that can be used in many ways. Combined with an unsettled heart, imagination can create angst and worry. But when combined with humility, a God-centered imagination can connect us with God himself.

Give it a try right now. Find a quiet place to escape — even the bathroom if you must, which is every parent's secret hideaway. Take some deep breaths and recenter your scattered senses upon God's immediate presence. Believe he is sitting there with you. Open your heart and ask the simple question, "What do you see when you look at me?" Then wait for the thoughts that seemingly bubble up or "pop" within you.

This simple process causes us to refocus on the Holy Spirit, who dwells within. Slowing down and voicing a simple prayer is an intentional act to give him the freedom to speak to us through this flow in our spirit. His living water flows within. You may find that as he speaks, a picture or short scene will play in your imagination. For others, words or fully-formed thoughts will be dropped into your frame of reference.

Whatever they are, make sure to jot down your impressions in a journal or on a piece of paper. There's a good chance what you receive is going to be deeply personal. It may even connect with your own story, drawing on past memories of that puppy you had in fourth grade or the wildflowers you see alongside the road while driving.

A few years ago, I taught a class on hearing God's voice. Towards the end of the evening, we set aside time to be quiet and to "tune in" to what God might be saying. There was a young woman in the class who had a beautiful vision. In her vision, she walked into an empty restaurant. No one was there except the waiter, who was standing on the other side of a large oak counter. The waiter was Jesus himself. He had a handlebar mustache that was waxed at the ends. Behind him were an assortment of bottles, filled with all manner of differently colored liquids. Jesus told her that if she was thirsty, he had a drink for her. Jesus could satisfy any thirst she could experience.

Hearing from God through this form of "seeing prayer" can be a powerful and transforming experience. It leaves you with a sense of being understood by God, having been encountered in a deeply personal way. Your interactions with God end up anchored in a story, a visual narrative that carries more meaning than words tend to convey.

Here is a picture of what I have experienced using this form of prayer. In this vision, I walked up to a workshop and found the door unlocked. I opened the door, walked in, and saw a muscular man wearing a leather apron. He had broad shoulders, strong arms, and rough hands. He was working on a boat. It was a woodshop. The craftsman looked up at me. As we exchanged glances, I knew it was Father God. A big smile came across his face. There was a set of blueprints tacked up on the wall behind him. It was for a boat he was making. I found myself fascinated by the blueprints. Instead of being written out with an ordinary pen or pencil, they had been drawn with golden ink.

He told me that I was this boat. He has been in the process of making me. I felt him tell me that I don't need to worry about the process or be concerned about the end result. He told me to rest in the fact that he knows what he's doing. He doesn't make mistakes. His rough hands are skilled and don't waver. What he intends to build in my life will surely come to pass.

Three Important Questions

As you tune into the flow of thoughts that are bubbling up from within, you should record your observations in the moment. Some people can remember better than I can. Those people may find they can simply listen and then come back later and reflect upon what they heard. I find it helpful to have a notebook nearby so I can jot down the impressions I receive. My brain can behave like a sieve, so I need to write things down.

Either way, it's important to capture what you receive. Using my earlier example, as I'm experiencing this vision, I jot down the following: "Entering the workshop. Blueprint with gold ink. Hands are strong." I'm writing down notes that include the most important data points I can see in the vision. I try not to stop midstream and analyze what I'm receiving; otherwise, I risk shutting down the flow of thoughts.

Capturing important details allows me to "test" that experience later. This is an important step. Your imagination, like a hammer, is a tool created for building. And just like a hammer, it must be used wisely.

After I have finished hearing from the Lord in this way, I look down at my notes and ask a few questions. First, "Does this reflect the character of God *as I know it today*?" Don't skip this step! Scripture is clear that "Jesus Christ is the same yesterday, today, and forever" (Hebrews 13:8). This means his character is consistent. His values remain unchanged. Feeling shamed, criticized, or discouraged are good reasons to exercise caution. However, feeling a sense of peace, love, or comfort are good signs pointing to God.

The second question to ask is related to the first: "Does this reflect the character of God, *as it is revealed in the Bible*?" We need to ask this question because faith in God rests on more than just personal experience. Developing a habit of reading Scripture, particularly the Gospels, will connect you with the ways of Jesus. Through the stories, you'll see how Jesus connected with people. He was compassionate (Matthew 9:36). He wasn't intimidated or turned off by human weakness and need (Matthew 8:1-4).

These two questions will help you test what you receive through "seeing prayer." These are personal questions to ask yourself. The third and last question to ask is, "What do you think?" This requires asking someone you trust and, ideally, someone who has *also* spent time listening to God in prayer. Receiving even a little bit of feedback can go a long way in developing confidence as you are learning to hear God's voice. We'll cover this more in a bit.

Getting It Right

I assume by now you're either ready to jump in and begin practicing, or you're terrified to make a mistake. Let me calm your fears. It's okay to make mistakes. God's acceptance of you isn't based on performance.

People ask me: "What if I hear wrong when I listen to God?" It's not a matter of *if* you will hear wrong. It's a matter of *when* you will hear wrong.

I think about how my youngest son recently learned how to ride a bike. He went through several stages of this learning process. At first, he was very disinterested in learning how to ride without training wheels. He begged us to keep the training wheels on his bike. Why? He didn't want to enter an uncomfortable situation.

But we told him, "No, Micah. It's going to be so much better. You're going to have so much fun. You're going to love riding your bike without training wheels."

At that point, he became more open to the idea. But he said, "Please hold me." He needed that extra stability. But it didn't take long before he was off riding by himself.

I really think it will be the same for you as you learn to hear God's voice. It's not going to take much before you have confidence. However, it's crucial that you not let fear stop you in this process. It's normal to make mistakes. There will be times as you're listening that you will make a mistake. So you must have a plan for when you fail. But remember that God is there to hold your hand. He's an excellent teacher.

> **THERE WILL BE TIMES AS YOU'RE LISTENING THAT YOU WILL MAKE A MISTAKE. SO YOU MUST HAVE A PLAN FOR WHEN YOU FAIL.**

There is this amazing story about how Peter the disciple walked on water. (Matthew 14). A terrible storm had developed on the Sea of Galilee. Peter, along with the other disciples, was battling crashing waves through the night in a tiny fishing boat. They were too far out at sea to swim to shore. They had to press on through the stormy night.

It was three o'clock in the morning when the disciples saw Jesus walking toward them *on the water*. They were tired before. Now, they were tired and completely freaking out. They thought they were hallucinating, or worse, a ghost had come to them out on the water.

Jesus spoke to them. He knew what they were thinking. "Don't be afraid," he said. "Take courage. I am here!" (Matthew 14:27).

All the other disciples thought Peter was crazy when he called out into the stormy night, "Lord, if it's really you, tell me to come to you, walking on the water" (Matthew 14:28).

What would have happened if Peter had never stepped out of the boat? What if he had never taken a risk? What if he had played it safe?

Instead, Peter was fearless. He acted first and reflected on his decisions later. He seized the moment. He was impulsive, but not reckless. Peter knew — or at least suspected — that his friend was waiting for him out on the chaotic waves.

I'm sure the other disciples could have given Peter ninety-nine reasons to stay in the boat. They would have all been based on logic and good "common sense," but they all would have come from a place of fear.

Peter walked on the water that night. Sure, there was a time when he took his eyes off Jesus and began to sink. He made a mistake in the process. But Peter walked on the water that night — not his fearful friends in the boat. And his reward? His reward was the experience of meeting Jesus beyond his fears.

You need to have a plan for when you fail, but don't let fear hold you back. Be like Peter and walk out to Jesus on the water.

Start Small. Focus on Yourself.

When you're just starting out and learning to hear God's voice, it's wise to begin by only listening for yourself. It can be tempting to try to get words from the Lord about friends or family. But this is one time where it's good to be self-centered. Why? Because if you do make a mistake and hear wrong, you're only affecting yourself.

As followers of Jesus, we need to be very careful in how we use the phrase, "I think God told me this or that about you." As soon as you say that, you're representing Jesus to someone else in an obvious way—and that's a responsibility best treated with caution. There's already a lot of misrepresentation of God's heart occurring in society today. You can represent Jesus best by taking the time to learn how to hear his voice for yourself first.

A second suggestion, similar to the first, is to avoid asking questions about anything too significant. Don't look to make any major life decisions at this point. Avoid asking if God wants you to marry this person or that. Don't let your first question be, "Lord, should I move to Africa?" A time will come to ask those questions, but not yet.

Focus on questions like, "Who do you want to be to me right now?" He may reveal himself as one who brings comfort or a defender you can run to in a crisis. You can also ask, "What do you see when you look at me?" These are questions of identity: Who am I? How does God want to relate to me in this season? What you hear will boost your confidence, draw you closer to him, and create a foundation for asking more directive questions.

The third thing you can do is to find a trusted person with whom to share your experiences. This is important. As I mentioned before, find someone who has a history of hearing God's voice. Little old ladies can be good candidates for this job. They'd love the opportunity to spend time with you. They might even bake you cookies! Do you have a praying grandma?

Trust that God will lead you to that someone with whom you can share your experiences and receive feedback. From my experience, people of prayer are often unassuming, grounded, and joyful. Look for those signs. If you can't find someone, reach out to me, and I'll try to help.

The fourth thing, and this one is often overlooked, is to read the Bible. I recommend that no one really begin this process of learning to hear God's voice unless they are going to commit to reading the Bible regularly. As a starting point, I strongly suggest you begin reading through the Gospels and become familiar with Jesus — the one with whom you'll be connecting.

You might catch someone refer to reading the Bible as "getting grounded" in the Word of God. What they mean by that is you'll be developing a solid understanding of God's character. Reading the Bible is more than just gaining facts; it's about getting to know a person. Psalm 103:7 talks about how "the Lord made known his ways to Moses" (ESV). There's something very different between knowing the facts about somebody and knowing their ways.

I know many facts about my wife. I know what color her eyes are. What her favorite flower is. What type of food she likes to eat. But real intimacy is found in understanding a person's ways, knowing their manner, knowing their character, and the way they operate. You can discover those things about God as you read the Bible and interact with him.

One last thing. You must have humility in this process. You will make mistakes. Learning to pray is a lot like riding a bike; everyone falls off a few times before they get the hang of it. If you share with someone else something you heard in prayer and they have some serious concerns, listen to them. Be open to coaching.

No one runs a marathon right out of the gate. As you practice, you will get better and will gain confidence. You can hear God's voice, but it may take some time to connect the dots and become familiar with the process. Have patience and enjoy the process.

Keep in mind the words of Oswald Chambers, who said, "Prayer does not fit us for the greater work; prayer is the greater work."[8] Prayer is not a means to an end. It *is* the end. Through prayer, we connect with God, the most brilliant, kind, and interesting person you will ever meet.

What If I Don't Hear?

As we draw this chapter to a close, I want to briefly cover one last question I often receive: "What if I don't hear from God?" To that, I say, "Don't get discouraged!" It's not a matter of ability — whether you have what it takes. You *can* hear his voice for yourself. Neither is it a problem with God. Like a fiery star in the night sky, always shining its light, the Father is forever speaking and revealing himself. It's in his nature. He can no more stop speaking than the stars can extinguish their brilliance.

Connecting with God cannot be reduced to an equation. There is no three-step process that works every time. But I will say this — if you want to go stargazing, you'd be wise to drive out to the country. Position yourself in the right place. Escape far from the city lights to see what has always been overhead. Here are a few possibilities to best position yourself to hear his voice.

Begin by asking yourself, "What's in my diet?"

Our culture today is overloaded with stimulation, from Facebook to Instagram, from Netflix to the nightly news. We're constantly bombarded with content. I can find myself so full of the things in my culture, that there's no space left inside my heart when it comes time to listen to God. He is speaking, but it's hard to take in anything more. I'm like a child who has ruined his appetite for dinner by snacking on chips.

If your "heart diet" is like I just described, you might want to take a break and do some cleansing. Commit yourself to a one-day pause from media "junk food." You'll be amazed at the things that you begin to hear. Make room in your life for God to speak, and you'll soon start receiving downloads.

Similar to the previous question, you can ask, "Is there anything for which I need to repent?" Repentance is a word we don't often hear in our world today. For some, it may trigger feelings of shame or judgment. However, the Bible doesn't frame repentance in those terms. True repentance means a change in direction. It's like spring cleaning for your soul. It's an action, not a feeling or an "I'm sorry."

If there is something in your life that the Holy Spirit has put his finger on? Perhaps you're still bitter at someone for the words they said. There may be a bad habit you know is destructive, but you don't want to stop. Refusing to turn away from those things could be why you are hitting a wall. It may be that God has *already* spoken, and he wants to remove that blockage with you — together — before moving on to something else. Repentance is a powerful tool through which to hear God's voice.

These are simply a few suggestions to keep in mind. Remember: This isn't a sprint, it's a journey. Invite God into your life. As you spend time persisting in his presence, you will begin to hear his voice. Remember the words of Jesus: "My sheep recognize my voice. I know them, and they follow me" (John 10:27 MSG). It may take time, diligence, and even repentance. Yet every moment spent is a moment invested. And those who engage in the pursuit to hear God's voice will never be disappointed (Romans 10:11).

Apply

Growth requires change. It's that simple. Throughout nature, we see the old adage proved true again and again: "If nothing changes, nothing changes." Every songbird has been pushed out of its nest. It's the only way its newly discovered wings can be put to use. All it takes is a little bit of courage and a nudge. The same is true for us. Through inward reflection, we discover our "wings," but it's only by application that we learn to fly.

Several suggestions for applying the truths from this chapter have been included below. This is not an exhaustive list. However, it should be enough to get you started. Find something that fits your personality. It should be action-oriented and push you just a little further than you feel comfortable.

- Escape from the busyness of life to find a quiet corner to "be," to just be present in the moment. I like to sit in my favorite blue chair before the sun rises, and always with a warm cup of coffee in my hand. In that place of silence, close your eyes and turn your focus toward God. Use your imagination to see the Father's face smiling at you (Numbers 6:25). Take a few minutes. Don't rush this process. When you are finished, record your experience below as a sort of written prayer to God. How did it make you feel to "see" God smiling at you? Were you surprised? Was it difficult?

_____

_____

_____

_____

_____

_____

_____

_____

_____

_____

_____

_____

_____

_____

_____

_____

_____

_____

_____

- Find your quiet corner once again. If I'm busy at work, I may take a few minutes to close my eyes and pop in my headphones. I like to listen to the "Deep Focus" playlist on Spotify. Try to put a smile on your face. It's incredible how a smile, even a forced one, can prepare your heart to hear from God. In that place of rest, imagine yourself standing next to Jesus, shoulder to shoulder, alongside a seashore. No one else is around. You can be authentic without fear of criticism or rejection. In this moment, express to him the things you are feeling. Record them below as a sort of written prayer. Why are you here? What do you want him to know?

- Having written your letter to Jesus, use your imagination to "see" yourself next to Jesus along the seashore. You turn toward him. His eyes connect with yours. You see the smile on his face (Psalm 119:135). Jesus takes the time to read your letter. He pours over every word, understanding the heart behind what you wrote. Now done with the letter, he looks up at you and speaks. At this point, "tune in" to the flow of thoughts in your consciousness and write down what you sense Jesus has to say back to you. Use the space below. If you get stuck, just refocus the "eyes" of your imagination on his face. Enjoy the process. Try this multiple times.

- Who do you know that prays? Is it your grandma, a neighbor, or that barista at the coffee shop who has a sparkle in her eyes? Whoever they are, write them a note and ask them to pray for you. Tell them that you're learning to hear God's voice. Invite them to check in on you to see how things are going. If you can't think of someone, reach out to me for suggestions.

FAITH:
Seeing and Believing the Truth

5

Relying on God has to start all over everyday, as if nothing has yet been done.
—C.S. Lewis

Faith does not operate in the realm of the possible. There is no glory for God in that which is humanly possible. Faith begins where man's power ends.
—George Müller

Faith is foundational to the life of the person who would follow Jesus. It's something that Jesus values. "When the Son of Man returns, how many will he find on the earth who have faith?" (Luke 18:8). Our faith is something that pleases him (Hebrews 11:6). Faith is the currency of God's kingdom.

But what is faith *really*? That's the crucial question. Nobody questions whether faith is important. Where people disagree is what faith looks like in action. Is it merely the power of positive thinking, or is there something more to it? It's a word that's difficult to define, both to the "churched" and to those who wouldn't consider themselves Jesus followers.

Faith is similar to the word "love" in the sense that it gets used everywhere. We hear about it on the radio. We see it on signs and billboards. We read about it in books. It shows up in country music. It's used to sell laundry detergent. And we use it to describe a relationship with God.

Surely we can't all be talking about the same thing. The word is used by so many people in so many different contexts that it has lost its meaning. So let's start with the basics and build from there.

Faith is defined as "assured reliance on the character, ability, strength, or truth of someone or something."[9] Is that vague enough for you? Faith is trust. We place trust in people and things daily. Even now, I'm trusting my wireless keyboard to work as I write this book; and it better not die on me like the last one did.

But even that definition doesn't go far enough. It doesn't clearly describe the kind of faith God values. For the life of a Jesus follower, faith is confidence in God. It is confidence in his intentions, that they are right; and his nearness, that he will answer when we call to him. True faith, faith that works, is all about placing our trust or confidence in the right place.

As a child, do you remember having bad dreams in the middle of the night? I remember waking up in a panic. My heart pounded as I cowered under my blankets. My mind would play tricks on me as I peered out into the darkness of my room. I feared the shadow monsters and creatures lurking under my bed. It was terrifying.

However, I believed everything would be okay if I could somehow run out of my room and down the hall to reach my parents' bed. I would eventually work up enough courage, throw my covers to the side, and race down the hall. I'd run past all the nasty things that lurked in the darkness and dive into their bed. Snuggled next to my parents, I immediately felt safe.

If I was close to my parents, everything would be okay. As a child, I learned quite early on to put my confidence in the character of my parents. They were close and willing to protect me.

Faith is not powered by mere positive thinking. You can't have faith in faith. Well, you can, but it will eventually let you down. I can "have faith" that I'll retire at an early age and live on the beach, collecting seashells. Doesn't everybody have dreams like that? But most of those dreams are never fulfilled because they're based on wishful thinking.

Neither does faith look like spiritual roulette, where the odds eventually swing in your favor—if you just hold out long enough—like that song by Journey, "don't stop believin." This is hardly different than buying lottery tickets as your retirement plan.

You have one life to live. Don't waste it on empty faith.

Empty faith comes from the world, not from God. It's a house of cards that topples as soon as your positive thinking gives way to doubt. You trusted in yourself, but you let yourself down. Oddly enough, it's ironic how people who live this way blame God when things don't work out as hoped.

> **YOU HAVE ONE LIFE TO LIVE. DON'T WASTE IT ON EMPTY FAITH.**

*(Problems + Pressure) * Time = Outcome*

Here is a math problem that is discouraging even for optimists. What a dismal outcome. It's like multiplying anything by zero. No matter how hard you try, no matter how many positive thoughts you decide to believe, you're never going to make progress.

There is a different type of faith, one that adds an additional variable into the equation: God himself. The faith God is looking for is tied to him, not to some ideal frame of mind or emotional state. It says, "I'm going to give up trying to control my life and instead let God run things for a while." It believes he is both willing and able to handle the challenges I'm facing (Psalm 138:8). This is the kind of faith that pleases God.

Many times, I'll find myself saying, "God, trusting you seems like the craziest thing to do right now. I have no idea how you're going to get me out of this mess. But I choose to believe that you've got this."

In this way of life, I can confidently believe "all things work together for good, for those who love God" (Romans 8:28 ESV), all the while juggling my doubts and uncertainty. It leaves the details for him to sort out, while I remain focused on following him in the day-to-day. It makes allowances for the One who is kind of heart and loyal to his promises. No matter what the situation produces, whether good or bad, he will be there with me, and his presence will always be more than enough.

His presence cancels out what I lack in myself.

More Than Enough

Jesus had a nickname for his disciples: "You of little faith." Those words comfort me. Why? They remind me that I am just as vulnerable to unbelief as those disciples who were closest to Jesus. Jesus accepted them despite their doubt, maybe even because of it. Unlike the religious leaders of that time, at least these men were honest about their lack of faith.

They were qualified to follow him because he had called them himself. And so they followed: full of doubts, fears, and misunderstandings. They came with all their emotional and spiritual baggage. They were a mess, yes, but they were the ones with Jesus. They responded to the same invitation that is extended to us.

On one occasion, Jesus and his disciples arrived at the shores of the Sea of Galilee, having just sailed from another place. A significant number of people had gathered to hear from Jesus and to have him heal their sick loved ones. There was a multitude. According to the accounts, there were five thousand men there that day, in addition to their families. Scholars believe the actual number could have been fifteen or twenty thousand people.

Having spent the whole day ministering to the people, the disciples suggested Jesus send them into nearby towns to buy food. "That isn't necessary — you feed them," he replied (Matthew 14:16). With one comment, Jesus placed the problem in their hands. And thus, their lesson in faith began.

Can you imagine the expression on their faces? "*Us*, feed *them*? Are you kidding?"

Remember our math problem? Problems plus Pressure multiplied by Time.

"The math just doesn't add up, Jesus!" They had five loaves of bread and two fish, which might as well have been a zero in their minds. In fact, I bet one of those men could have eaten that much food for his lunch alone. No matter how you move the numbers around, anything multiplied by zero is still zero.

You were living the good life in the morning, drinking your iced caramel macchiato on the way to work, the morning sun shining in a blue sky. Life was good until you were yelled at by your boss, found out a friend had died or received a discouraging call from the doctor. Everything is suddenly thrown out of balance. Immediately, you were aware of your need. Have you ever experienced a moment like this?

The disciples were holding this small lunch, their "nothing," and instantly were mindful of their need. Positive thinking wasn't going to feed twenty thousand people. So much for faith in faith, right?

Jesus motioned with his hand and said, "Bring them here" (Matthew 14:18). He was unphased by what little they had to offer. The lesson continued, and you better believe his students were paying attention.

He blessed the "nothing" and told them to begin handing it out. The food was multiplied. It was a miracle. Everyone ate

JESUS WILL TAKE THE LITTLE YOU HAVE AND MAKE UP FOR WHAT'S LACKING.

until they were satisfied, and even then, there were still twelve baskets of food remaining. It was a sign to the disciples: Jesus will take the little you have and make up for what's lacking.

He was teaching them about faith. But they didn't get it. How do I know? Because not long after this event, they came across another multitude who needed to eat. Jesus drew a crowd because people began to realize he was near and willing to meet their needs.

This time, Jesus spent three days with the crowd. They brought to him people who were lame, blind, crippled, those who couldn't speak, and many others. He healed them all.

On the third day, Jesus shared with his disciples, "I feel sorry for these people… I don't want to send them away hungry, or they will faint along the way" (Matthew 15:32). He was testing them. Here comes lesson number two.

Once again, the disciples were fixated on what they were lacking. ("You of little faith.") Once again, Jesus multiplied the little that was there, and there was more than enough. This time seven baskets of food were left over. It was another sign: Bring your little to him, along with all your doubts, and he will not only meet your needs but also produce a surplus.

Lesson number two, and they still didn't get it! How do I know? Shortly after this occurrence, Jesus and his disciples traveled across the Sea of Galilee and landed on the other side. The disciples realized they hadn't brought any bread for the journey. This time, the disciples indeed had nothing.

They did what came most naturally. They began arguing with one another.

"Jesus knew what they were saying, so he said, 'You have so little faith! Why are you arguing with each other about having no bread? Don't you understand even yet?'" (Matthew 16:8-9).

He had been teaching them about faith all this time.

It mattered very little what the disciples had at that moment, whether it was just a little or nothing at all. What mattered was who they were with. The faith we're talking about puts confidence in God's ability to provide.

"And this same God who takes care of me will supply all your needs from his glorious riches, which have been given to us in Christ Jesus" (Philippians 4:19).

God invites us to bring him our "nothing" and to be honest about what we lack. Bring your doubts and unbelief. Don't try to hide them. Your "five loaves of bread and two fish" don't intimidate him, because he will always be more than enough.

> **IT MATTERED VERY LITTLE WHAT THE DISCIPLES HAD AT THAT MOMENT, WHETHER IT WAS JUST A LITTLE OR NOTHING AT ALL. WHAT MATTERED WAS WHO THEY WERE WITH.**

The greatest gift God can ever give you is himself. Everything else will eventually run out, just as the bread did for the disciples. But faith connects us to Jesus, who will always be more than enough.

Regardless of the struggles and hurdles you are facing, Jesus himself is more than enough. You don't have to walk alone, and you can trust him with the outcome.

Leave the outcome to him who can effortlessly multiply the fishes and the loaves. Release your need to control the situation, and believe that he really will cause "all things work together for good, for those who love God" (Romans 8:28 ESV).

Seeing Rightly

Several years ago, a friend of mine was driving her daughter to school. It was a beautiful, sunny morning with barely a cloud in the sky. Her daughter turned to her and said, "Mommy, I wish there was a rainbow outside." Her mom agreed, being polite, but not giving it much thought.

"As a matter of fact," her daughter said, "I'm going to ask God to send me a rainbow." She rolled down the car window and shouted at the top of her lungs, "Jesus, will you please send me a rainbow?" She rolled her window back up and settled into her seat. She was confident the rainbow would come, even though the sky was still blue and there was no rain in the forecast.

They finally pulled into the school parking lot. My friend turned off her engine. As they got out of the car to walk into the building, her daughter gasped. My friend ran over from the other side of the car to find her daughter standing over a dirty water puddle in the parking lot. She faced downward, but her expression of delight could not be hidden.

"Mom! Jesus sent me my rainbow!" she said.

Motor oil mixed with water had produced a rainbow effect of beautiful colors in the parking lot. It took the perspective of a child to see what God had done. Jesus had sent her a rainbow. Faith requires seeing from the right perspective.

To follow Jesus means to enter a new way of doing life. It's not only the expectation of a life to come— as if all our hope were in a heavenly mansion in "the sweet by and by."

> **FAITH REQUIRES SEEING FROM THE RIGHT PERSPECTIVE.**

Neither does he remove all the obstacles in our way. Instead, he invites us to allow him to redefine our outlook on life. And that process is all part of a faith lifestyle.

It is as Charles Swindoll said: "I am convinced that life is 10% what happens to me and 90% how I react to it."[10] Your perspective will determine how you react to life.

Perhaps that's why Jesus said to have faith "like a child." Children have no preconceived notions about the world. They behold everything with wide-eyed wonder. They have not lived long enough to see the world in negative terms, like "He can't," "He won't," or, "It's not possible."

Every situation is filled with imagination and hope in the extraordinary. Knights slay dragons. Locked doors always have a key. There's still a trap door to escape from the bad guy.

You can live into a childlike faith by embracing humility. Humility keeps an open mind and accepts that you may not have all the details. It tries to avoid making judgments or filling in the blanks with negativity. It makes room for Jesus in every struggle and allows him to own the outcome.

You can never know with certainty how or when God will answer. But answer he does, though not always as you'd expect. Stop claiming you know the best way for God to fix your problems. You may not be seeing God's answer, and it's right in front of you. He may be making rainbows on the ground as your eyes are fixed on a cloudless sky.

I didn't start wearing glasses until I was in high school. Before that time, I thought everyone had difficulty seeing the teacher's notes on the board. I didn't realize how bad my vision was until I could see with 20/20 vision. My whole world was changed by having a new perspective.

It's the same with faith. Too many people walk around blind, and they don't even know it.

A lifestyle of faith looks more like nurturing a friendship than it does like getting your problems solved. There's an old adage in the church that says, "We seek his face, not his hand." It's loosely based on what Jesus said in Matthew 6:33, "Seek the Kingdom of God above all else, and live righteously, and he will give you everything you need."

Faith grows best in the mundane, when no one is looking. It responds to constant care and feeding, a little at a time, for the long haul. It grows as you spend time with God.

> **FAITH GROWS BEST IN THE MUNDANE, WHEN NO ONE IS LOOKING.**

Make yourself aware of his presence as you drink your morning coffee. Turn off the radio as you drive home from work and share your hopes and doubts with him. Read or listen to the words of Jesus in the Gospels. Come to him with brutal honesty, saying, "I don't get how all this works, but I'm going to trust that you are good and that your commitment to me is solid."

Take a deep breath and exhale. He's got this, and you belong to him.

Recognize: Your faith is a gift from God. He is the "founder and perfecter of our faith" (Hebrews 12:2). He gives you faith, and he will nurture that faith in your heart. You've been set up to win. In fact, you've been given an unfair advantage, which is the sure promise that he will make up for whatever you lack.

But every morning, just as with my glasses, you must correct your perspective to reap the benefits. Putting glasses on once is not enough. Faith must be applied continually.

Some days you will find yourself surrounded by negativity. The storm will feel so close. At those times, you must stop and readjust your vision. Bring your weak faith to him, no matter how insignificant it may seem, and let Him multiply it.

Don't Just Sit There!

Faith is the conviction that Jesus himself is more than enough. No matter how impossible the problem, he's present in your midst and is willing to meet your need. As you invite him into your crucible, one of the first things he loves to do is upgrade your perspective.

Reality gets redefined through his lens of hope. He drives out pessimistic thinking, which is filled with words like "never," "can't," and "won't," and replaces it with possibility. Faith transforms our mountains into anthills, and makes us aware of God's towering presence overhead, relieving our feelings of being vulnerable and alone. That's why Jesus said, "Anything is possible if a person believes" (Mark 9:23).

Moments such as these are precious. They remind us to "be still and know" that he is God (Psalm 46:10). In the chaos, I can hold these convictions within and intentionally rest from my striving to control the world. This is good for us—we get to learn dependence and to allow him to be strong on our behalf.

Yet, at some point, this type of faith must produce movement. Belief without action is good for trivia nights and radio contests, but little else. If I am convinced that he is more than enough for me, then I am required to do something about it.

I've never seen my lawn mow itself. No one else can work out at the gym on my behalf. The same is true for my walk with Christ. Don't just sit there! I can't always hold my hands out and wait for deliverance, and neither can you.

Faith can't be lived out on the sidelines. It's meant to be applied as you follow Jesus out into the world, the one with that troublesome neighbor or stressful work environment.

Faith can often look a lot like work. But it's work coming from a different place. It doesn't strive as if it all depends on my own efforts. After all, it is faith in his abilities, not mine.

"For we walk by faith, not by sight" (2 Corinthians 5:7 ESV). The emphasis here is on walking. Your faith must eventually be translated or expressed into action in your life. That's why James 2:20 reminds us that "faith without good deeds is useless."

So is it faith, or is it works? The answer is yes. It's not one or the other. You need both. It's faith that works. "Because I believe I take action." Faith is all about movement. It refuses to accept defeat. However, it comes from a place of rest.

The faith God values works from a place of rest. Rest is a state of being where I content myself in knowing that God is overseeing the struggle I'm facing. He will sort out the details as I continue to move in the direction he reveals.

Abraham (then Abram) modeled this kind of faith when God told him, "Leave your native country, your relatives, and your father's family, and go to the land that I will show you. I will make you into a great nation" (Genesis 12:1-3).

What a request! God asked him to pack up everything he owned and hit the road, even though Abraham didn't know where he was going. His journey led him from ancient Turkey to Israel, a distance of six hundred miles. How would you like to make that trip on foot? Abraham needed to see his crisis through a different lens and maintain that perspective as he literally walked his road toward the promise.

A lifestyle of faith is a dance. God moves on our behalf so that we might move in response. We each have a part to play; it's a back-and-forth. Isn't that the basis of a healthy relationship?

God promised to make Abraham into a great nation. Abraham's part was to "Leave... and go to the land" that God would show him. It wasn't enough for him to simply believe God's promise. His faith was proved genuine by stepping out.

Reflect

A LIFESTYLE OF FAITH IS A DANCE. GOD MOVES ON OUR BEHALF SO THAT WE MIGHT MOVE IN RESPONSE.

Setting aside time to reflect allows us to become more aware of our inner selves and what God may be showing us. It's like a shopping mall directory, searching for the "You are here" arrow. Reflection helps us to understand where we are and where we want to go.

Allow your heart and mind to think about and process what we covered thus far, paying attention to your inner feelings, questions, and even frustrations. During reflection, we create space for God to search our hearts and expose things that were previously hidden. This results in an authentic connection, both with God and ourselves.

- Think about your life and the challenges you are currently facing. Are you in a situation where, like the disciples, all you can see is what you lack? The mountain may seem too high to climb, or the road may feel much too long. Write down two or three of those struggles below.

_____

_____

_____

_____

_____

_____

_____

- As you review the struggles listed above, what kind of feelings are associated with them?

_____

_____

_____

_____

_____

_____

_____

- Faith believes that Jesus is more than enough to handle the challenges you face. Ask the Holy Spirit if he is bigger than the struggles you're facing. List each one out by name. You might find it helpful to pray, "Holy Spirit, what would you like to give me instead of these feelings I wrote out?" For example, instead of anxiety, he may want to give you peace. Write down what you hear below.

_____

_____

_____

_____

_____

_____

_____

_____

- Together with the Holy Spirit, play the "What if…" game. Pick at least one of your existing challenges and reword it so that it's filled with hope and potential. Rely on your notes from question three. It looks like this: "Holy Spirit, what if you are using my difficult job situation as a way to produce tremendous peace in my life?" Write your statement down in the space below.

_____

_____

_____

_____

Purpose in the Trial

It was hard to breathe. I was carrying a fifty-pound backpack filled with all my clothes and essentials for a three-month trip to India. We were in the north, in the foothills of the Himalayan Mountains. My team had been on a trek for five days. The views were surreal during the day, and the nighttime sky was blanketed with stars, unlike anything I had ever seen.

We were preparing to climb the largest mountain we had so far encountered. On the other side of that mountain would be lush, high-altitude meadows, dotted with sheep and tiny villages. We were on our way to visit people in those communities who knew nothing about Jesus. We had flown across the world to teach them English and to show them God's love in tangible ways.

One step, then another. The team began to climb the steep trail toward the mountain pass. My breathing was heavy underneath the load. The air gets quite thin at 20,000 feet above sea level. The weather was cold, and snow flurries had already begun to cover the ground. Our guide was a Nepalese man who was probably no more than five feet tall. His dark skin had been weathered by years of leading Westerners through the mountain passes that he called home.

He signaled for us to follow him. Then, as if a gun had been fired at a track race, he quickly took off up the path. His pace was impressive and effortless. We, on the other hand, were still getting acclimated to the thin air of that mountain place. Our eyes watched as he nearly ran up the path to a point, probably about a half-mile away. He sat down on a rock and lit a cigarette. Here we were gasping for air, and he was smoking!

My team did eventually reach that mountain pass. We greeted our guide. We were so happy to be done with the climb and to rest our legs. I struggled to keep myself coherent and not pass out. Our guide was smoking his third or fourth cigarette, enjoying the view of the mountain meadow that stretched out before us.

We reached our destination, but to get there, we had to climb the path set before us. There were no alternative routes. The trial almost seemed too great, but we had no other choice. There was no turning back. We had left civilization days ago, and the opportunity for which we had come so far was waiting for us. This was my mountain trial.

You will encounter trials in life. This is an unavoidable truth. We all know what it's like to discover you're in a situation that is undesirable, uncomfortable, and inconvenient. It stretches out before you like a foreboding mountain path.

No matter what stage of life you're in, no matter your gender or education or financial status, we all have trials to face. Just like my mountain path, we face trials where there is no turning back. The only way forward is through the discomfort before us.

Your trial might be externally visible. Perhaps you have been out of work for some time. You feel the pressure to put food on the table and maintain appearances with your friends and family.

Your struggle may be less visible, like depression or discouragement. Perhaps you struggle with self-hatred or bitterness toward a friend or family member. Your trial may be a person; it seems like whatever they do, they rub you the wrong way.

It is impossible to avoid trials in this life. However, my promise to you is that there is a purpose to the trials you are facing — if you will embrace them. You will discover a blessing — on the other side, and usually not before. This is the first secret to developing a lifestyle of faith.

When I was younger, I thought that I was pretty selfless. I had a rather high opinion of myself and my ability to meet the needs of others. All that changed when I had kids. Suddenly there was someone new in my life who took away my sleep in the middle of the night. He changed my priorities. I used to steal away and watch my favorite TV show or grab a few minutes to read a book. But now those precious moments were hard to find. Changing diapers and burping babies became the new normal.

Of course, I love being a dad. I have four boys of my own, so apparently, the setbacks I encountered weren't enough to deter me from adding to our family. However, I bring this up to emphasize the fact that trials, whether seemingly good or bad, will produce discomfort. And it's discomfort that exposes our weakness.

I don't like to be weak. I like to be strong and capable. I like to be self-sufficient and self-directed. But my experience has taught me great rewards are found on the other side of your discomfort.

Nobody enjoys experiencing weakness. When I go to the gym, I don't necessarily enjoy working out and pushing myself with movements that I'm not good at. When we're exposed to discomfort, our first reaction is often a desire to run away.

Our Western culture places too much value on comfort and entertainment. As soon as trouble comes across our path, our knee-jerk reaction is to want to flee. But the truth is that you cannot run from your weaknesses forever. Indeed, you may run from the situation for a time, but before long, it's going to find you. It may look slightly different, wrapped in a different scenario, or delivered by different people, but the trial will return.

People today seem to be obsessed with discovering their purpose in life. A casual look at any book kiosk in the airport will prove this point.

People want purpose and destiny, and movement. And all of that is available to those who follow Jesus. However, those things are usually discovered on the other side of your trial.

Those are the things that you find out as you walk by faith, hand-in-hand with Jesus. This challenges our belief in delayed gratification. I know that most of my boys would rather accept a giant chocolate sundae right now than receive twenty dollars one month from now. "A bird in the hand is worth two in the bush," goes the proverb. We want fast-food solutions, but God often has something else in mind.

God's big-picture intention is that we might "be conformed to the image of his Son" (Romans 8:29 ESV). The Father wants to make you look and act and be like Jesus. Before the resurrection comes the cross. Even Jesus, the perfect and unique Son of God, had to be perfected through his suffering (Hebrews 2:10).

On this journey in life, Father God is taking us along the path toward a destination, which our strength cannot lead us to. The trials we encounter reveal our weaknesses and bring us to the end of ourselves and our own strength. It's scary to be in a place like that. It can be terrifying to feel vulnerable and weak. It's hard not to have all the answers. Yet the sooner we realize our weakness, the sooner we can begin to draw on him and actually start taking steps down the path that he has laid out for us.

There is a purpose for your trials — if you will allow it. "God causes all things to work together for the good of those who love God and who are called according to His purpose" (Romans 8:28). There's not always a good reason why storms arise, but we can trust in God's desire and ability to redeem those difficult circumstances for our good. If we give ourselves permission, we can begin to see our trials as preparation for our next upgrade in God. Trials are the soil in which faith grows.

Faith Grows through Testing

God uses trials to grow your faith. I live in Minnesota. As I write this, outside, it's below freezing with several feet of snow. They tell me one day spring will come, but it's hard to believe them. We'll eventually pull out our gardening tools and prepare the ground for planting. However, we'll never be able to grow oranges, bananas, or avocados. The climate and soil just aren't suitable for it. In the same way, faith can only be produced in the soil of our trials.

Faith is grown during a season of testing. Just like with gardening, there are no shortcuts to produce faith overnight. It can only be produced as part of a longer process.

During my time in India, as we journeyed through the Himalayas, the only way we could reach our destination was to walk down the path that had been laid out before us. It takes courage to embrace the trial that is set before you. But be comforted in the knowledge that God is not looking for you to take a leap of faith. He's looking for you to take a small step. And then another. And then another, until you reach the other side of the trial.

This type of prolonged obedience and delayed gratification can test our resolve. On the one hand, it can be challenging to trust God and continue walking in the same direction. But he journeys with us every step of the way.

A lifestyle of growing in faith is a lifestyle of being engaged with God. The path may be steep, but he walks alongside you. You may not be able to see more than a few steps ahead, but Father God guards your way, and he knows the road well. There will be times when your faith fails. You will trip on some metaphorical rock. You'll become offended at God or at somebody else. You'll think thoughts you shouldn't think.

You'll do things you know you shouldn't do. But our Father God is one who loves redemption. He loves to use our failures to expose our weaknesses and, in that place, prove his faithfulness to us.

The Apostle Paul said that even when we are faithless, God remains faithful (2 Timothy 2:13). To grow in faith is to know weakness. But it's also an opportunity to encounter God's abiding presence on the path we are walking. Weakness can produce dependence, which is what God wants. And the goal of the journey is that we would decide to lean on him for our strength and come out the other side having learned how faithful he is.

There's a beautiful picture in the Song of Solomon of the bride and her bridegroom. After several invitations earlier in the story, she finally decides to get up and follow him into the unknown. Toward the end of the story, she reappears, coming up from the wilderness, leaning on her beloved bridegroom (Song of Solomon 8:5).

God Values (Small) Faith

Faith is potent. Jesus said even having the faith of a mustard seed, though tiny in size, would be enough to make a massive impact (Matthew 17:20). There are times when you'll be hard-pressed to find that faith. You might feel discouraged, as I have felt when rummaging through my wife's purse looking for our car keys. "They have to be *somewhere!*" There is a bit of doubt mixed with the hope that the answer is within reach.

Amid the trial, you may feel like the disciples whom Jesus called, "you of little faith" (Matthew 8:26 ESV).

> **SIMPLY COME TO GOD WITH YOUR FAITH, REGARDLESS OF HOW LITTLE YOU SEEM TO HAVE, AND ASK HIM TO INCREASE IT.**

Only one thing is needed: Just don't give up. Simply come to God with your faith, regardless of how little you seem to have, and ask him to increase it.

God is the strong one in this relationship, not you. He's not looking for self-sufficient followers. While we hope our children grow up to be independent, Father God intends that we might find our strength in him. Growing in faith will produce more dependence on him, not less. His encouragement to us is, "Follow me. Find your strength in me. Come close and hold my hand."

This self-admission of weakness, and our consequent running toward God, is precious in his sight. It is precisely what he desires. The Apostle Peter knew much about weak faith. Having followed Jesus for three years, Peter abandoned him in his final hours before he was hung on the cross. "Woman, I do not know him," he told bystanders emphatically. Peter was a coward during his time of testing. But he didn't remain there, and neither should you.

Perhaps it was because of this heart-wrenching denial that Peter, when he later reflected on his life, wrote, "the tested genuineness of your faith, more precious than gold that perishes, though it is tested by fire may be found to result in praise and glory and honor at the revelation of Jesus Christ" (1 Peter 1:7).

Stumbling faith is not the complete absence of faith. You are guaranteed to fail, but the failure doesn't mean your faith is invalid. God is not done with you. You may have given up on yourself long ago, but God never will. It's just another opportunity to review the material and to try again.

You can hold belief and unbelief in your heart at the same time! As a man once said to Jesus, "I believe; help my unbelief" (Mark 9:24 ESV). Your faith may be small, but it is real. And that makes it precious to God.

You are on a journey over many mountains. And the ultimate goal is to attain connectedness with God. Scripture says that God looks at us and remembers that we are dust (Psalm 103:14). He remembers our frailty. Your weakness does not disappoint him. Instead, it becomes an opportunity through which to discover his faithfulness and strength.

I eventually reached the top of that Himalayan mountain pass. My lungs finally gained composure, and stars were no longer in my vision. I looked out and saw the beautiful mountain meadow lying before me. There were tiny villages filled with beautiful people I was eager to meet. The guide who ran ahead of me leisurely sat on a nearby rock, smoking a cigarette.

I have found that the Holy Spirit walks by my side through every trial. I'm never alone. And his voice to me always says, "You can do it! One more step. Keep going! I believe in you. Rest on me. Hold my hand." And he is saying the same thing to you — if you would have the ears to hear it.

Apply

Growth requires change. It's that simple. Throughout nature, we see the old adage proved true again and again: "If nothing changes, nothing changes." Every songbird has been pushed out of its nest. It's the only way its newly discovered wings can be put to use. All it takes is a little bit of courage and a nudge. The same is true for us. Through inward reflection, we discover our "wings," but it's only by application that we learn to fly.

Living by faith requires two types of application. The first step involves coming to a place of inward peace or rest by adjusting your perspective. Sometimes the obstacle in your life doesn't need to be removed; you just need the ability to see it from a different angle. Once you see from God's perspective, the one always filled with hope and purpose, the problem becomes a steppingstone to further growth and spiritual wholeness.

Yet it's not enough to simply see things rightly. We need to adjust our lifestyle in such a way that it responds to this new perspective. There's a difference between knowing the truth and living into the truth. This second step of application seeks to embrace and answer the difficult question, "What am I going to do about it?" You need both parts — perspective and action — to see true transformation. When those complementary parts are combined, you'll experience an acceleration in your life and the transformative momentum that accompanies a lifestyle of faith.

Step One: Seeing the Truth

- Reflect on the struggles that are most pronounced in your life. You may find it helpful to ask yourself the question, "Is there any area of my life that's generally lacking in hope?" Write down your insights in the space below, along with any associated feelings. For example, "I am worried about finding a job to provide for my family," and the associated feelings might be, "Worry, restlessness and fear."

_____

_____

_____

_____

_____

- Take a few moments to connect with the Holy Spirit by recognizing his presence in your life and speaking to him. You may find it helpful to say, "Thank you for being here with me in the midst of my struggles."

- When you feel ready, you're going to ask the Holy Spirit to help you connect the dots between the way you're feeling and the underlying root cause. As my friend Richard Sicheneder likes to say, "If there is a fruit, there is a root." The root will often be a lie that you have believed about yourself, about God, or about others. You may find it helpful to ask the Holy Spirit, "What is the root of this? Where is this feeling of worry coming from?" In this example, I may hear the lie, "I am the only one who will look after my needs. I am alone." Write down your insights in the space below.

- Once you have gained some insight into this root, you can move on to replacing the lie with the truth. That is the essence of true repentance. It's a change of direction, from believing (and living into) something false to believing (and living into) something true. Ask the Holy Spirit, "What is actually true about my situation?" In this example, you may write, "Am I *actually* the only one who will look out for my needs, or is there someone else?" In this example, you may hear the Holy Spirit say to you, "I've got this. You don't have to worry about the outcome." Write down your insights in the space below.

_____

_____

_____

_____

_____

_____

_____

- What's left to do at this point is to respond in thankfulness. You need to own the insight you received, even it feels uncomfortable or awkward to embrace in the moment. It can take courage to believe something new. In this example, you may respond in prayer by saying, "Thank you for taking care of me and delivering me from all my worry. I choose to trust and leave the outcome to you."

Step Two: Living <u>into</u> the Truth

Once you've received the truth, you must live into it. This is what the Bible calls the "renewing of your mind" (Romans 12:2 NIV), where you "let God transform you into a new person by changing the way you think" (Romans 12:2). You reject the lie, accept the truth, and allow the Holy Spirit to rewire your brain. Here is one example of how you can put your faith into action.

- Using your notes from Step One, craft at least one affirming statement about yourself. In this example, "I am not alone. God takes care of my needs." Write this down on a notecard or in a note on your phone. Speak this truth to yourself every morning. Do it several times. This is not merely the "power of positive thinking," where people arbitrarily speak truisms to themselves. This is intentionally coming into agreement with God's thoughts until you begin to think them for yourself. Repeat them daily until you find your heart agrees with them.

- While embracing God's perspective for the situation, ask the Holy Spirit how you can partner with him. It's important not to fall back into old habits or practices that were rooted in the lie. You may find it helpful to pray, "Holy Spirit, what simple step can I take today to follow you?" Don't worry about what you accomplish on a to-do list. It's more important to adjust to following him from a place of truth. Write down your insights in the space below.

OBEDIENCE:
The Joy, Not the Burden

6

There will be no peace in any soul until it is willing to obey the voice of God.
—D.L. Moody

Maturity comes from obedience, not necessarily from age.
—Leonard Ravenhill

No one has to teach a child to like being in control. It just happens naturally. As soon as we realize we have choices, that we can eat ice cream instead of salad, we get hooked. We want to be the ones who choose. We like being in control.

As you grow older and gain more responsibility, you find yourself in situations, whether inside your family, your community, or your work environment where you are in charge. You're the one who gets to decide what you eat for lunch. You're the one telling people at work what to do. You're the one calling the shots.

We get so used to being in control of our own choices that the idea of obedience can be tough to accept. It can make us question whether obedience to God is optional. Just like the crowds in Jesus' day, it can be hard to hear the words of the Master, "If any of you wants to be my follower, you must give up your own way, take up your cross daily and follow me" (Luke 9:23-24).

In this lifestyle of following Jesus, there will be times when we are led in a direction different than what we expected. It may not feel comfortable or be easy going. But to those who will accept it, obedience is the narrow path that leads to a deeper life. It is the treasured secret that the great saints of old knew of and embraced. Eric Liddell, the great Scottish Olympic gold medalist and Christian missionary, had this to say about obedience:

> Obedience to God is the secret of spiritual knowledge and insight. It is not the willingness to know, but willingness to DO (obey) God's will that brings enlightenment and certainty regarding spiritual growth.[11]

On our journey together, we've explored the joy found in connecting with God through prayer and partnering with him through his indwelling Spirit. We've looked at walking by faith and seeing things from a different perspective. All these concepts are foundational to a lifestyle of following Jesus. Obedience, however, is where we reach a crossroads. Something is required of us. As it has been said, "If Jesus is not Lord of all, then He is not Lord at all."[12]

You may be tempted to ask, "What right does God have to tell me how to live?" I'm reminded of my time spent teaching Sunday school to a group of preschoolers. There was always that one kid—the one who stands there and gives you "the look" when asked to do something. Regardless of the request, he plants his feet, crosses his arms, and, with a furrowed brow, spits out the words, "You're not the boss. Why do you get to tell me what to do?"

I chuckle at the memory. Many times I find myself identifying with that young kid. God spoke to me, but it was not what I wanted to hear. He's invited me into obedience, but I don't want to obey.

In this chapter, we're going to look at obedience through a different lens. Instead of viewing obedience as a mere set of demands, we're going to see it's part of something much bigger called "covenant." A covenant is an arrangement that is made between two parties. It's like a contract, but with more weight to it.

Marriage is the covenant with which we're most familiar. It brings together the benefits and responsibilities found in a committed relationship. Healthy marriages produce an environment of love, acceptance, stability, and the joy of being deeply known. Nothing else compares. But it all comes at a price, paid by patience, humility, and laying down your own rights for the sake of someone else.

Throughout history, God has initiated covenants with human beings. We see it all over the Bible. There was the covenant God made with Adam and Eve in the garden: "Be fruitful and multiply. Fill the earth and govern it" (Genesis 1:28). There was the covenant made with Noah following the flood: "Never again shall there be a flood to destroy the earth" (Genesis 9:11 ESV).

God made a covenant with Abraham: "Look up into the sky and count the stars if you can. That's how many descendants you will have!" (Genesis 15:5). This all came at a time when Abraham was old and had no children.

God made a covenant with his people at Mt. Sinai: "Now if you will obey me and keep my covenant, you will be my own special treasure from among all the peoples on earth; for all the earth belongs to me" (Exodus 19:5).

In our present day, we can enter a new and better covenant through the death and resurrection of Jesus (see Hebrews 8:6). "And all of this is a gift from God, who brought us back to himself through Christ" (2 Corinthians 5:18). It is all-encompassing. The former covenants, while good in previous times, had to be replaced by a better one, a perfect one. There is no need for improvement. When we are brought into this covenant relationship with God, we gain access to all the joys and benefits of that relationship through obedience.

Speaking of this perfect covenant, God says: "But this is the new covenant I will make with the people of Israel. On that day, says the Lord, I will put my laws in their minds, and I will write them on their hearts. I will be their God, and they will be my people" (Hebrews 8:10).

These covenant vows, "I will be their God, and they will be my people," are very similar to how a man and woman get married. In exchanging vows, they give themselves to one another. What is mine becomes yours, and what is yours becomes mine. "For richer or poorer, in sickness and in health…"

All of these benefits are from God for us. We receive his protection. We receive his provision. We receive his faithful promise, knowing that "He will neither fail you nor abandon you" (Deuteronomy 31:6). We receive the joy of knowing him and the blessing of being known by him. We reap all the benefits of a covenant relationship with God. Yet, obedience is how we respond to his generosity and the covenant God has made with us.

Take My Yoke Upon You

"Come to me. All of you who are weary and carry heavy burdens and I will give you rest" (Matthew 11:28). Here is the covenant blessing offered to us by Jesus. Do you have heavy burdens? Are you weary? If so, come to Jesus, and he will give you rest. What a benefit we receive from him!

But what does God want? What does the covenant require of me? Jesus goes on to say: "Take my yoke upon you. Let me teach you because I am humble and gentle at heart, and you will find rest for your souls. For my yoke is easy to bear, and the burden I give you is light" (Matthew 11:29-30).

Back in those days, long before John Deere tractors, a farmer would plow his field using oxen. His method was simple: pair an experienced ox that had worked the fields for many years with a younger, less-experienced ox. The old and the new would be connected using a wooden yoke. The young ox would submit his strength to the wisdom of the older ox, who would follow the lead of the farmer and guide the younger ox in the direction he needed to go.

As we enter this binding covenant with Jesus, he invites us to connect ourselves to him. It's not done by force. We're invited to willingly take his yoke upon us. And it's in this teaming together that we learn from him. We enjoy the blessing by walking alongside him, following his lead.

As we walk through life, there will be times when he will draw us in one direction or another. It's during those times our commitment to the covenant will be challenged. He may speak to your heart, sending gentle conviction about a TV show you're watching or how you're talking about somebody else in a negative way. You'll feel the Holy Spirit rising up within, giving you a little nudge to stop. This is what it looks like to be led by Jesus, to take his yoke upon yourself and allow Him to guide you.

When I was growing up, I'd often see bumper stickers on the back of cars that said, "Jesus is my co-pilot." Here's the truth: Jesus is not interested in being your co-pilot. He has his eyes on the pilot chair. He asks you to sit down next to him and enjoy the ride. Go with him always, but never as the leader. Enjoy the safety found in being a follower.

This type of obedience, the kind that pleases God, is always expressed in the context of relationship. In this place, you'll hear him saying, "This is the direction I'm headed, and I want you to join me." It's an invitation to partner, but it is on his terms, not yours.

The idea of turning over control can be scary. What if God turns out to be a taskmaster? A slave obeys out of fear. Many people relate to God in this way. They obey out of fear that something worse may happen to them. There is a big difference, however, between slavery and the invitation God offers us.

God is not looking for slaves. He's not even looking for servants. In fact, heaven is already filled with "millions of angels ministering to him" (Daniel 7:10). If God has an entire heaven full of angels, many millions of servants, what could he be looking for in you?

He's looking for partnership. He wants to journey together with you.

To Look Like Jesus

In 2 Corinthians 5:15, we read, "[Jesus] died for everyone so that those who receive his new life will no longer live for themselves. Instead, they will live for Christ, who died and was raised for them."

Christians back in the day used the term "absolute surrender," which meant laying down your will and desires and allowing God to rearrange your priorities. Now that you have been brought into his family, you've entered a covenant with him. He wants to change the way you live—for the better—but it requires having a surrendered heart.

We've come to God to enjoy all the benefits of a relationship with him, but he also has plans for us. "For God knew his people in advance, and he chose them to become like his Son" (Romans 8:29). Another place in the Bible refers to this as his "eternal plan" (Ephesians 3:9-13). His overarching goal is to cause you to mature and look more like Jesus.

I don't enjoy running. In fact, I like to joke with people and tell them that if you see me running, I'm either chasing someone or being chased by someone. Through the sweat, the aches, the discomfort, one thing cannot be denied—a lifestyle of exercise improves health and increases my chances of a long life. During long workouts, I have to remind myself of this. It's worth the sacrifice. I'm committed to the long-term outcome.

Walking closely to Jesus in obedience produces gains so much more significant than any sacrifice you will make. "For our present troubles are small and won't last very long. Yet they produce for us a glory that vastly outweighs them and will last forever!" (2 Corinthians 4:17).

When the race is long, believe God has a higher plan for you. Obedience is a discipline that, like running, may require you to walk through some momentary discomfort. The momentary testing is worth the long-term beauty he's producing in your life. God has one primary focus for your life—to make you look like Jesus. He wants to see your soul so thoroughly healed and nurtured that every day you look and feel and love just a little bit more like himself.

As with any kitchen remodel, the designer will produce a mock-up of how the finished kitchen will look. That design eventually gets translated into building schematics, which then get translated into the tasks that are done to produce the outcome. With any remodel, there is demolition involved. There is rebuilding. Before the final product can be enjoyed, there is a great deal of messiness.

You carry inside you the building blocks that will one day express the character of Jesus. Some of those building blocks are more hidden than others, hiding under a heap of insecurities, lies that we have believed, and addictions. But take heart. This call to obedience does not exist to serve his own selfish needs. God intends to see us transformed into someone whole and healthy—someone beautiful.

What Obedience Looks Like

Where do we look for an example of how obedience should be lived out? By now, you should know the answer. Jesus is our model. "Those who say they live in God should live their lives as Jesus did" (1 John 2:6). We're going to briefly look at two scenes in Jesus' life that are like bookends on his ministry.

The first scene is found in John 6:38. Jesus says, "For I have come down from heaven to do the will of God who sent me, not to do my own will." At the beginning of Jesus' ministry, we see he understood and embraced obedience. He came to accomplish the desires of his Father.

This statement is quite something, given the fact that just before this, Jesus had fed the five thousand (John 6). He took a few loaves of bread and a few fish and quite miraculously multiplied them and fed a multitude. "When Jesus saw that they were ready to force him to be their king, he slipped away into the hills by himself" (John 6:15).

Here is Jesus, God in the flesh, the rightful king of all, living out his obedience before the Father. The people see an opportunity to install him as their earthly leader. What would you do if a multitude rallied around you and wanted to make you their leader? Would you be tempted to rethink God's plan for you? Who wouldn't want to set aside a path of suffering for a shortcut to glory? What a difficult decision to be made!

What do we see Jesus do? He slips away into the hills by himself. Jesus shows us that there will be times when obedience to God asks you to say no to an opportunity, even when saying yes looks much more appealing.

How did Jesus know what to do in this situation? Jesus had cultivated a connection with his Father long before the trial. The questions of obedience had been tested in his heart again and again. He was able to resist when a seemingly great idea presented itself. He knew it wasn't what his Father wanted. It wouldn't have been the type of kingship the Father had for him.

For Jesus, the long-term reward of obeying the Father and honoring the covenant was more important than the short-term benefit. He would have gained a crown, but not the one the Father had prepared for him.

The second example we see is found the night before Jesus was crucified in Mark 14. In that passage, we see Jesus in the garden of Gethsemane. It's late in the night. All Jesus' closest friends have accompanied him to the garden, though they've all fallen asleep. He's there in the garden, and he's weeping all alone. He knows the suffering the next day will bring.

He cries out to his Father, "Everything is possible for you. Please take this cup of suffering away from me, yet I want your will to be done, not mine" (Mark 14:36).

Jesus was saying, "Father, you know what is best for me, and I'm going to trust you." There are times God asks us to say yes to the path ahead, even when saying no looks much more appealing.

He knew about the beatings that were ahead. We can only imagine the pain he felt from the whip on his back, time after time. In the end, he submitted his very life to the will of the Father, allowing himself to die on the Cross. He chose to obey in the moment and trust the outcome to his Father. All this, while knowing full well that he could have called down ten thousand angels to come to his rescue (Matthew 26:53).

Jesus modeled obedience that wasn't forced. It was birthed out of a heart that trusted the ways of his Father. And it wasn't mindless obedience. It allowed for human emotion. There was real wrestling his soul in that garden, the night before his death. "Could there be another way?" he asked in anguish. There was no other way.

"Will you trust me?" That question had been settled long before that night. Obedience looks like trust in the face of extraordinary circumstances. Jesus trusted the Father, come what may.

"I have given you an example to follow. Do as I have done to you. I tell you the true slaves are not greater than their master. Nor is the messenger more important than the one who sends the message. Now that you know these things, God will bless you for doing them" (John 13:13-15).

Reflect

Setting aside time to reflect allows us to become more aware of our inner selves and what God may be showing us. It's like a shopping mall directory, searching for the "You are here" arrow. Reflection helps us to understand where we are and where we want to go.

Allow your heart and mind to think about and process what we covered thus far, paying attention to your inner feelings, questions, and even frustrations. During reflection, we create space for God to search our hearts and expose things that were previously hidden. This results in an authentic connection, both with God and ourselves.

- When we make a commitment to follow Jesus, we are brought into a covenant with him. In this covenant, we access all the rights and privileges afforded us. What are a few benefits that God provides you for which you are thankful?

_____

_____

_____

_____

_____

_____

_____

_____

- God wants to provide for your needs. This involves replacing your heavy burdens with ones that are light and more easily managed (Matthew 11:30). Are you carrying any heavy burdens in your heart? What issues are weighing you down or stealing your joy?

_____

_____

_____

_____

_____

_____

_____

_____

- Jesus said, "Come to me... and I will give you rest" (Matthew 11:28). We must come to him to experience his rest. In the last few weeks, have you been intentional about drawing near to God regularly? What has that looked like?

_____

_____

_____

_____

_____

_____

- Sometimes we avoid drawing near to God for fear of what we will lose. Is there anything God might be asking you to give up? Most fear is rooted in irrational thinking. Remember the words of Jesus: "If you cling to your life, you will lose it; but if you give up your life for me, you will find it" (Matthew 10:39). You might find it helpful to pray, "Holy Spirit, is there anything in my life that you'd like to remove and replace with something better?"

_____

_____

_____

_____

_____

_____

Mistakes to Avoid

In the last year, one of my boys has taken an interest in baking. My family doesn't eat much sugar, so I wonder if this newfound hobby is a cleverly disguised way to eat more sweets. Time will tell. Nevertheless, we found ourselves with a handful of bananas that had survived long enough to get overripe. The time had come for another baking project.

So what do you do when you have overripe bananas? You make banana bread. My son was adamant about wanting to read the instructions and bake the bread on his own. He gathered the ingredients, mixed them up, and placed them in the oven. When the bread was done, we noticed two things: it was unusually dense and incredibly sweet.

The sweetness did not surprise me. My boys have not yet learned that too much sugar can be a bad thing. However, the denseness of the bread is what did surprise me! I asked my son how he made the bread. The recipe told him to mix various ingredients in separate bowls. Only then should everything be combined. Noah thought that step was unnecessary. Instead, he threw all the ingredients into a single bowl. It was the fastest approach.

Although the banana bread was gobbled up that day, it taught my son a lesson: There is a right way and a wrong way to make banana bread. The same is true when it comes to obedience. There is a right way to obey and a wrong way. Let's look at a few ways that people approach obedience incorrectly.

There are two mistakes that people commonly make when it comes to obedience. The first mistake is attempting to produce obedience in your life by sheer grit and determination. Try harder! Dig deeper! This method relies entirely on self-effort. People with even the best intentions can end up living this way. They're convinced that the most important thing is the outward result. But this type of obedience ignores what is going on in the heart. Willpower, as we all know, eventually runs out.

Remember, Jesus said, "My yoke is easy to bear, and the burden I give you is light" (Matthew 11:30). Sharing the same yoke, the same load, is a reminder that obedience is something done in partnership. If the burden you're carrying is awkward and burdensome, perhaps it's not coming from God. Listen for his voice through prayer. Either you took on something that wasn't for you, or you need to see the "burden" with the right perspective.

God loved you and *accepted* you when you were at your very worst. Romans 5:8 reads, "But God showed his great love for us by sending Christ to die for us while we were still sinners." This can be difficult for some to receive. Ironically, it can be more comfortable to rely on self-effort and perform for God's acceptance. However, the truth still remains: You don't need to perform for his affection. May God give us the grace to believe this!

All of these practices—prayer, faith, obedience, and the like—come down to a single point of focus: it is all about nurturing a relationship with God and being intentional to connect with him daily. That's why, in the passage about the yoke, Jesus tells us to draw near. "Come to me, all of you who are weary and carry heavy burdens, and I will give you rest" (Matthew 11:28). There is no alternative. When I stand before the Lord one day and look into his eyes for the first time, I want to recognize his gaze. I want to see memories in those eyes.

The second mistake people make is thinking their obedience needs to be perfect to be genuine. I imagine them having this kind of mental wall calendar in their mind, marking off each day as a success or a failure with a big red sharpie. But all it takes is just one juicy piece of gossip or someone to cut you off on the highway, and instantly an animal rises up within you. You curse at the driver in front of you. You spread that scandalous rumor. Suddenly, you've blown it. You feel like you've failed.

Shouldn't we know by now that perfection is unattainable? Why is it that we hold onto this ideal? I think it comes out of immaturity, a misunderstanding of who God is and what he values. We can carry around a fear of failure, a fear of disappointing God. For some of us, we've incorrectly thought that he wants perfection at any cost.

Living in this type of all-or-nothing mindset is a sure way to set yourself up for discouragement. The worst thing you can do when trying to live a life of obedience is to live with an unrealistic standard of perfection.

> **GOD IS NOT LOOKING FOR A FLAWLESS PERFORMANCE. BUT HE DOES VALUE THE DIRECTION IN WHICH WE ARE HEADED, AND HE WANTS US TO KEEP MOVING, NO MATTER HOW MANY TIMES WE DO A FACE-PLANT.**

"The godly may trip seven times, but they will get up again" (Proverbs 24:16). God is not looking for a flawless performance. But he does value the direction in which we are headed, and he wants us to keep moving, no matter how many times we do a face-plant.

Afraid to Disappoint

As I mentioned earlier, I served in an organization called Youth With A Mission (YWAM) in my early twenties. For three months, I lived in an apartment complex in Jacksonville, Florida, with other students my age. Everyone there was sincere and wanted to know God more deeply and be equipped to follow him in their lives.

Most mornings, we would handle breakfast on our own, and then gather in a classroom for our studies. One morning, as I was walking to class, I saw one of my classmates standing in the middle of the parking lot. He was standing still, not moving a muscle. I didn't think anything of it at the time, because I didn't want to be late. However, once the class started, I became keenly aware that my friend was not in his expected seat. Five minutes passed. Ten minutes passed. Eventually, my friend showed up and sat down. "Dude, why were you so late?" I asked.

He told me that the night before, he had told God he wasn't going to do *anything* unless he specifically heard the Holy Spirit speak to him. His heart was sincere, and he genuinely wanted to obey God. So the next morning, when he woke up, he didn't just roll out of bed. He waited until he felt what he believed was God telling him to get out of bed. This waiting continued as he got dressed, ate his cereal, and walked outside his apartment. He found himself in the parking lot.

He stood there for a long time because he was waiting for God to give him directions—to continue walking to class. He stood in the hot sun for fifteen minutes! Silence. No voice from heaven. No inner prompting to go this way or that. He finally gave up.

That story makes me chuckle. Don't allow your life to be directed by a fear of disappointing God. Obedience is more complex and deeply nuanced than being entirely surrendered to him or not. Surrender will be easy for you in certain areas of life, but there will be other areas that, no matter how hard you try, you'll struggle to trust.

It's important to celebrate the little successes and, in the face of defeat, to get back up and run to Jesus. God values your sincerity, even if you feel like you're stalled in an empty parking lot.

Every Door Unlocked

As a younger man, I believed God got frustrated at me—even angry—for my failures. I felt like they disqualified me from being loved by him. It would take several days of me walking in guilt and shame until I felt as if I had paid the penance for my wrongdoing. Suffering for acceptance. What a miserable way to live!

One day, I came across a passage of Scripture that changed the way I viewed my failures. "If we are unfaithful, he remains faithful. For he cannot deny who he is" (2 Timothy 2:13). In the face of disobedience, our God keeps his promises. Despite our failures—and sometimes willful disobedience—he remains faithful to us. That should get your attention, scandalize you even.

Your failure does not disqualify you from following Jesus. He doesn't put you in a time out. His love remains steady even when we are not. But don't stay there! Don't settle for less. Obedience, just like the other practices in this book, is a practice that you never fully graduate from. You just get better at doing it.

Ask yourself, "Am I following Jesus more closely today than I was before?" It's best to ask this question on a

> **"AM I FOLLOWING JESUS MORE CLOSELY TODAY THAN I WAS BEFORE?"**

weekly or monthly basis. You'll drive yourself crazy if you get too laser focused. "For he knows how weak we are; he remembers we are only dust" (Psalm 103:14). Make sure you're never more critical of yourself than God.

As you grow, you will open yourself up to more and more of God's influence in your life. Now, I'll find myself walking through a challenging situation and sense the Holy Spirit speaking to my heart, asking, "Will you trust me? Will you open the door to this area of your life?"

Now, I wish I could tell you how easy it is to respond with a yes. I'd be lying. It can be really hard. But my goal is to trust more often than not. I'd rather posture my heart rightly and fail a few times than reject his offer.

I like to see my inner self as a house with many rooms. Some rooms are closer to the front door. These are areas into which I can easily provide God access. There are no locks. In some cases, there isn't even a door. He has free reign. He can remodel and improve those areas as he desires.

Shortly beyond those front rooms, however, there is a hallway leading to areas in the back that may be dimly lit. Those rooms have doors that are closed, locked, or even nailed shut. It's more difficult to give God access to those areas: hidden sin, lies I believe about myself, areas of compromise.

The Holy Spirit may have already highlighted those areas in your life. You tried to keep him in the foyer, but he decided to explore. He's in the hall and knocking on the door that you've nailed shut.

God creates beauty wherever he goes. He remodels the hidden and darkened areas with ease, particularly those in which hope has vanished. He removes doors and tears down walls, anything to remove the barriers between him and us. And wherever he goes, he fills those spaces with light.

It can be a bit unnerving to give God the freedom to walk the darkened hallways of your heart. After all, what might he discover? May God give us the grace to trust in his kindness, remembering where he has said, "I am humble and gentle at heart, and you will find rest for your souls" (Matthew 11:29). God is looking for people who will say, "Though this looks impossibly hard, I will trust you."

Learning to Trust

Hudson Taylor was a missionary to China in the 1800s. He spent fifty-one years in that country, caring for the poor and campaigning against the opium trade. Known as a man of faith and prayer, Taylor once famously said, "God uses men who are weak and feeble enough to lean on him."

This is part of the irony of God's kingdom. "For when I am weak, then I am strong" (2 Corinthians 12:10). When we trust in his character—that he is loving, patient, kind, gentle—it becomes easier to obey. There are no shortcuts. In fact, obedience grows best in the soil of trust.

"God is working in you, giving you the desire and the power to do what pleases him" (Philippians 2:13). I love this verse because it reminds independent people like me that I am not alone in my growth journey. God is at work. Willpower will eventually come to an end, but his strength is limitless (see Psalm 147:5).

His intention is to produce within you the desire to do what pleases him. And this will happen as you connect with him. This requires some intentionality. You have to do more than just *want* connection. You have to make it a priority. Adjust your schedule. Turn off the television. Don't just want it — go after it!

Jesus described obedience using the concept of abiding. "I am the vine you are the branches," and again, "Abide in me" (John 15:5). Think about a grapevine. A branch doesn't need to do much to produce fruit. It just effortlessly draws its strength from the life that is in the vine. In our lives, this power comes from the Holy Spirit himself. As we spend time in his presence, he will quite naturally live out his desires through us. But you must be connected to the source!

As you prioritize time to connect with the Father, you will find him giving you the desire and power to do what pleases him. The fantastic thing is that the more you listen to him in that place of abiding, the more you'll discover that he has thoughts and opinions about your life. You will find him say, "This is what's important right now," or, "I want you to trust me with this issue you're dealing with."

Slowly, you'll become more aware of his kindness, which will produce in you a desire to trust him. This often occurs in short fleeting moments, peppered across the mundane of life. During those times, ask him questions, talk to him, become aware of his abiding presence. He'll prove himself to you—if you give him a chance.

"Rest in the Lord and wait patiently for him" (Psalm 37:7 KJV). As you grow in trust, you'll find that you can rest in the midst of uncertainty. This is because your state of being is not based on the outcome of the situation. It's based on the presence of him who never leaves you or forsakes you. With each small victory, there is a cumulative effect. Each success results in a little deposit of trust made within. With each victory, you'll find you're able to trust him more completely.

Apply

Growth requires change. It's that simple. Throughout nature, we see the old adage proved true again and again: "If nothing changes, nothing changes." Every songbird has been pushed out of its nest. It's the only way its newly discovered wings can be put to use. All it takes is a little bit of courage and a nudge. The same is true for us. Through inward reflection, we discover our "wings," but it's only by application that we learn to fly.

Several suggestions for applying the truths from this chapter have been included below. This is not an exhaustive list. However, it should be enough to get you started. Find something that fits your personality. It should be action-oriented and push you just a little further than you feel comfortable.

- A lifestyle of obedience should be built on the foundation of a healthy relationship. What are you doing to be intentional to prioritize time to connect with God? Spend a few minutes looking through your weekly schedule. Where in your week can you reserve time to pay attention to what he might be showing you? If you're just getting started, pick a ten-minute slot each day when you can slow down and be present with him. Write it down below or add it to the calendar app on your phone. Treat this time like you would any other appointment.

_____

_____

_____

_____

_____

_____

_____

- In the Reflection section earlier in this chapter, you asked the question, "Holy Spirit, is there anything in my life that you'd like to remove and replace with something better?" You may already know what it is. For example, maybe the Holy Spirit showed you that you were watching too much Netflix. Now is your opportunity to make some changes in your life. Spend a few minutes contemplating how you might live differently. Keep in mind that whenever we give up something at his request, he always replaces it with something better. Write down your commitment below and stick to it!

- Look at the diagram of the house below. Notice how there are some areas close to the entry door that are easily accessible. There are also other areas further away that can be hidden behind a closed door. Imagine your life as a house and the Holy Spirit standing at the entryway. Spend a few minutes reflecting on your life. Write down some areas of your life in the spaces below. Which ones are more accessible to the Holy Spirit's input? Which ones are currently off-limits?

You might find it helpful to refer to the list below during this exercise.

- Career/Business
- Finances and Wealth
- Friends and Family
- Recreation and Entertainment
- Health and Fitness
- Love Life and Sexuality
- Insecurities and Fears

Visit www.themattberry.com/house-worksheet for a printable version of this image.

- Now that you have filled in the diagram, spend a few moments looking it over. Ask the Holy Spirit, "Which area of my life would you like to occupy next?" Pay attention to an area that stands out to you. Be courageous and trust that any area he works in will ultimately bring about beauty. It will also, sooner or later, produce joy in your life. If you don't feel a specific area standing out, just pick one. Circle it on the diagram above and write in the margin, "God wants to fill this area of my life."

- Spend some time in quiet contemplation about the area of your life you circled in the previous step. You may find it helpful to ask the Holy Spirit, "Is there anything in this area of my life that you would like to change?" Jot down some ideas that come to you. Dialogue with the Holy Spirit about them and pick something that can be changed. Write it below as a reminder.

_____

_____

_____

_____

_____

_____

_____

_____

LOVING OTHERS:
Becoming Kindness to All People

Following Jesus is simple, but not easy. Love until it hurts, and then love more.
—MOTHER THERESA

Love pays attention. Love listens to the fears and the doubts of others and treats them with respect. Love accepts others the way Jesus accepts you.
—RICK WARREN

This chapter is about adventure. God's invitation is always accompanied by the opportunity to discover something new: about him, about yourself, or about someone else. Whatever way it comes, there is a joy to be found on the journey. Perspective is important, and we need a new one if we are to live our lives in the way of Jesus (1 John 2:6).

Jesus said to enter his reality, what he called his "kingdom," we must receive it as a little child (Mark 10:15). This is ironic. It's not the grownups, the sensible and safe, who receive his gifts. We are invited into a lifestyle of simple trust and confident expectation. And God gives us permission to play and to seek out adventure with him.

This invitation is for any person who would know God at more than just a surface level. There is a side of God that can only be discovered by leaving our comforts and pursuing adventure. He is always present with me, but in another sense, he's "out there," away from what is predictable, tamable, or safe. This part of him can't be discovered by reading a book. Neither can it be found on our own terms. His presence is to be found among "the highways and hedges" (Luke 14:23 ESV) as we go out into the world on mission with him.

In John 1:14, it says that Jesus "became human and made his home among us." Another author paraphrased it this way, "[Jesus] became flesh and blood, and moved into the neighborhood" (John 1:14 MSG). He became one of us. The beauty of the Christmas story is that God left his comfort zone, set out on an adventure, and came near to us.

Jesus was fully God before that first Christmas. He existed with the Father and the Holy Spirit in the mystery that we call the Trinity, extending into eternity past. But when the right time came, the Father sent his Son in the likeness of our human frame (Galatians 4:4).

We certainly weren't looking for him. Humanity, even back then, was lost and broken beyond repair. There was an aching void inside. We needed help, but we lacked the awareness and the language to articulate what we needed to fix the problem.

Jesus came to us as part of a rescue mission. He was like Seal Team Six, sent into inhospitable conditions behind enemy lines, with a set of mission objectives. He came to those who were his enemies, to those who were broken. And his mission? He "came to destroy the works of the devil" (1 John 3:8) and "set free all who have lived their lives as slaves" (Hebrews 2:15). That's you and me! We were slaves to the devil because of our sin, trapped in our own arrogance, hatred, jealousy, and hopelessness.

Through this rescue mission, God revealed his truest motives toward us. He came to rescue us. He showed us a love that expresses itself at any cost. "For this is how God loved the world, He gave his one and only son so that everyone who believes in him will not perish but have eternal life" (John 3:16-17).

The mission was successful. He ransomed us from the kingdom of darkness (Mark 10:45), making it possible for us to be adopted into his family and filled with his Spirit. We who were captives were recruited to join his mission, which continues to this day. "As the Father has sent me, so I am sending you" (John 20:21). Though Jesus died for all, making it possible for everyone to enter this new life of hope and meaning, not all know. He has sent us to be his love—expressive, accessible, and extravagant—to those around us.

My wife is gorgeous, both without and within. It was only two weeks into our friendship that I was convinced. I didn't want to live without her. I drove to Sam's Club down the road and picked out a ring. Being in my early twenties and without much semblance of a career, I didn't have much money to spend. However, I bought the most expensive ring I could afford. I literally emptied out my bank account. I bought a costly ring because my wife was worth it. She had to know how much she was worth to me.

In the same way, the Father gave his only Son for you. This is the kind of costly love he has for lost and broken people. "The Son of Man came to seek and save those who were lost" (Luke 19:10). He knew the path that would lie ahead for his Son. He knew Jesus would be brutalized and killed on a cross. But he still said, "They're worth it." His extravagant love proves just how much you are worth to him.

Love In Action

During his earthly ministry, Jesus spent his time with people you wouldn't expect. Though he is the "King of kings," he didn't socialize with the political elite. Though he is the "Lord of lords," he didn't entertain the religious leaders of the day (See 1 Timothy 6:15). Jesus sought out ordinary people, including those who were broken, downtrodden, and marginalized. He didn't avoid the victims; quite the opposite: He gave them a place to belong.

When criticized, his response was, "Healthy people don't need a doctor—sick people do. I have come to call not those who think they are righteous, but those who know they are sinners and need to repent" (Luke 5:31-32).

Jesus wasn't turned off by people's brokenness. If he were with us today, he would be eating with the refugees. He would be found comforting those sold into sex slavery. He would be sitting with the drug addict, listening to lonely, and having a barbeque with your next-door neighbor.

It's been nearly two millennia since his feet walked our earth. Technology has changed. Nations have risen and fallen. Yet God's character and priorities remain the same. Today, through the Holy Spirit, God is still going out, leaving the comfortable places to meet people where they are.

Theologians refer to this concept as "prevenient grace," which means that God has "gone before." The Holy Spirit is *already* at the gas station down the road. He's *already* in your neighbor's house. He's *already* working in the lives of the people around you. He has loved them from the beginning.

God's presence is not restricted to so-called "holy spaces." He isn't inhabiting our church buildings throughout the week, "holding up the fort" while the rest of us are off living our lives. Neither is he waiting for you to carry him out to "dark places." He is already there. There is no place where he is not. That is good news!

The Index Card

My wife has a colorful personality. A few years ago, she picked up a pair of flashy sunglasses with rainbow-colored lenses. They're shaped like hearts. How's that for making a statement? She doesn't wear them just for fashion; she wears them as a reminder to see people the same way that God views them, through the eyes of love.

Each person is a work of art but caught somewhere in the middle of the process. The paint is still drying in places. Some colors just don't seem to blend together. There are portions of the canvas still unfinished. It all looks disjointed.

To the artist, however, the canvas holds a masterpiece not yet revealed. The artist can see the beauty beyond the momentary imperfections. That's good news for you. It's also good news for those around you. God has no intention of giving up on any us. The Father wants to change your perspective, whether or not you use rainbow-colored heart glasses.

Several years ago, I worked for a tech company in the Twin Cities. My shift began very early in the morning. I had one other coworker who worked the same hours. His name was Dennis.

The two of us could not have been more different. I was in my mid-twenties, only recently having graduated into adulthood from a very safe and predictable Christian family. Maintaining appearances was important to me. I dressed my best to let everyone know I was serious about my career.

Dennis, on the other hand, was in his late forties. He had gone to Berkley School of Music to study the bass. He was incredibly artistic. He had a dirty mouth, but a sharp wit and an outrageous sense of humor.

Perhaps my funniest memory about Dennis is that he would wear these raggedy, old, button-up shirts — only buttoned halfway. He'd leave the top portion open, exposing a forest of chest hair. He looked like he was ready for a piña colada and a day at the beach. There were many occasions when I asked myself, *How on earth did this guy get a job here?*

I really wanted to connect with Dennis on a deeper level, but we literally had nothing in common. One evening on my way home, I found myself praying for him. As I was praying, the Holy Spirit spoke to my heart.

"Do you want to know how I see Dennis?" he asked.

It was a simple question, but profound. It had never crossed my mind that God would see Dennis differently than I did. I spent a few minutes in silence, listening for God's voice.

Several images flashed through my imagination: Dennis jamming with his bass, his boisterous laugh, and infectious smile. The Holy Spirit showed me that Dennis saw beauty in everything. I felt God impress upon my heart a few simple words, "I love that about him." So I grabbed a three-by-five index card and jotted it down.

The next morning, I went to the office with my scribbled message from God. Dennis's faded red Chevy truck was in the parking lot. Dennis had arrived before me. My stomach was in knots as I rode the elevator up to my floor. What would he think? I exited the elevator and walked down the hallway.

Dennis greeted me with a toothy grin. I mustered up the courage and blurted out, "Hey, Dennis. I was praying for you last night, and I felt like God showed me a few things about you. You want to know what he said?"

The expression on his face was a mixture of shock and something else I had not expected—curiosity. He was not expecting this as the topic of this morning's conversation. *God would have thoughts about me?* Having heard the question, he had to know the answer.

He leaned forward in his chair. He seemed hungry. Perhaps he hadn't known it or hadn't had the words to articulate what he felt, but in that moment, he seemed to know that what I had was something that he desperately wanted. "Go ahead," he said.

So I pulled out the index card and handed it to him.

There was a deafening silence as he stared at the card. Tears began to well up in his eyes. "You find beauty in everything you see. I love that about you, Dennis, and I just wanted you to know that. Love, God."

These were the words his heart had been longing to hear. Later on, he shared how he never felt permission to think of God in this way. The action seemed like such a small thing, just a few words scribbled on paper. But even a tiny seed can birth a forest.

The message on that index card changed him. From that day forward, Dennis and I shared a special connection. I began to tell him about Jesus—not just facts, but my own experience. We eventually began reading the Bible and praying together during our breaks. Dennis eventually made a decision to follow Jesus. I baptized him in the pool at his apartment complex. It was the only baptism I've attended that has been celebrated with blackberry currant martinis—his idea. It was certainly something worth celebrating.

The Lost Lamb

In Matthew 18, Jesus tells a story about a shepherd who has a hundred sheep, and one of them wanders away. Poor sheep. Poor foolish sheep. When the shepherd realizes what has happened, he leaves the other ninety-nine on the hills unattended, exposed to the elements and predators, to search after the one that is lost.

The story is scandalous. The mission is seemingly a fool's errand. The man's friends would have called him irresponsible. In simple economics, recovering the one sheep was not worth the risk of exposing all the others. Any sensible businessman would know that. "At least I have the rest of them. I'll recoup my losses next season when the lambs give birth."

But the shepherd in this story is far from ordinary—and that's good news for us—because we are each like that lamb stuck in the thicket, exposed to danger, and without hope. But Jesus, the Good Shepherd, is on his way. He will not rest until you have been found.

This story shows us how God has a different formula for determining value. A person's value is not based on what they have or can produce, but rather how deeply they are loved by God.

All kinds of people, the tired, exploited, confused, and discouraged, they all wanted to be around Jesus. They already knew the junk in their lives. No one had to inform them. They weren't looking for another critic with an action plan to fix their problems. In Jesus, they found someone who saw in them what they could not see themselves.

Jesus saw gold when he looked inside them. He wasn't intimidated by their mess. He saw beyond the shame, the addiction, and the hopelessness. And while these obstacles seemed insurmountable to them, to Jesus, they were easily overcome. "So if the Son sets you free, you are truly free" (John 8:36).

Think about the people you see every day: neighbors, coworkers, workout buddies, waiters, your family. These are the people God has intentionally positioned around you. And each of them is loved by God. We are invited, by the Good Shepherd (John 10:11), to seek after them even as he does. We are entrusted by God to love his precious ones and introduce them to the Jesus who has been pursuing them all their lives.

As you begin looking around your workplace and neighborhood, expect there to be gold hidden beneath brokenness. Ask the Holy Spirit to help you see with the right perspective. If not you, who else will see gold in your neighbor? Who else will stop the barista at the coffee shop and give them an encouraging word? Where else can people go to be told who they are and how they are seen by the God of heaven? The world is hungry for a different perspective, and you, through God's love, can offer that to them.

Reflect

Setting aside time to reflect allows us to become more aware of our inner selves and what God may be showing us. It's similar to a shopping mall directory, searching for the "You are here" arrow. Reflection helps us to understand where we are and where we want to go.

Allow your heart and mind to think about and process what we covered thus far, paying attention to your inner feelings, questions, and even frustrations. During reflection, we create space for God to search our hearts and expose things that were previously hidden. This results in an authentic connection, both with God and ourselves.

- Think about the people with whom you regularly interact, whether in your neighborhood, at the office, or in other spaces. What are their names? What do they look like? Take a minute or two to think about these people.

_____

_____

_____

_____

_____

_____

_____

_____

- Ask the Holy Spirit to highlight two or three of those people in your mind. Which of them, in particular, stand out? You might find it helpful to pray, "Holy Spirit, show me who of those in my circles could benefit most from feeling loved by you." Write down their names below.

_____

_____

_____

_____

_____

_____

_____

_____

- Without the help of the Holy Spirit, how do you usually view these people? For example, do you see them as hardened, disinterested, or problem cases that are too difficult to tackle? Use the space below to make some notes.

_____

_____

_____

_____

_____

_____

_____

_____

- Take some time with the Holy Spirit to work through your notes. As you feel led, use this as an opportunity to repent of this kind of negative thinking. Keep in mind that repentance is less about saying you're sorry and more about committing to changing your direction.

_____

_____

_____

_____

_____

_____

_____

- Lastly, ask the Holy Spirit to help you begin to see these few people the way he sees them. You might find it helpful to pray, "Holy Spirit, show me the gold that you see in _____." Use the space below to take some notes.

_____

_____

_____

_____

_____

_____

_____

_____

No Strings Attached

Shortly after we had moved to the country, my wife and I began praying for our neighbors. Some of them know Jesus. Some of them don't. But regardless of how they'd self identify, we believe each of them is loved by God. I often pray the Lord's Prayer on their behalf: "May your Kingdom come soon. May your will be done on earth, as it is in heaven" (Matthew 6:10). I expect to see beauty as God's Kingdom comes into their lives.

As we prayed for our neighbors, we noticed love for them began to grow in our hearts. This was ironic because we had no history with these people. We didn't even really know more than their names. But God did. He was keenly aware of every laugh, tear, unmet expectation, and future dream. As we prayed, he put his love for them in our hearts.

God's love produced a frustration within. I found myself asking, "What should we do with this love?" The question was on my mind several times throughout the day. Not having a clear direction, we decided to keep praying. God's love is expressive. Sooner or later, the answer would come.

One spring morning, my wife was walking by my neighbor's garden and saw that her garden hadn't been planted yet. This neighbor had some health challenges at the time and wasn't able to get down on her knees to care for her garden. My wife, Elisa, offered to get her garden ready for planting. I'm not sure how my neighbor replied, but there was probably some "Minnesota nice" in there—that polite friendliness with an aversion to conflict. Regardless, the matter had already been settled in Elisa's mind.

The next day, she took our boys to the neighbor's and put them to work. Together, they cleared the weeds and planted some seedlings, various vegetables, and flowers. They had a blast—and our neighbor watched from her deck, taking it all in.

There's a surprising amount of joy to be found in loving simply for the sake of love. Just because. It feels wonderful to love someone with no strings attached. We didn't see our neighbors as a project or as people who needed fixing. They were simply people deserving of love!

That backyard garden did end up producing beauty. But the greater harvest was found in the lives of our neighbors. They're now good friends. Our kids refer to them as "Grandma Betty" and "Grandpa Gene." Betty gives some of our boys reading lessons. Gene builds rockets and invites everyone over to help launch them. We've seen God's Kingdom come in their lives. It produces so much beauty, and it's a blast to watch.

Life can be painful. When we're exposed to criticism or cruelty, our hearts can shrivel up like a stale raisin. We respond to hurt by building walls to protect ourselves. There is a way to reverse it, though. God's love, when planted intentionally and generously, always produces a harvest. It doesn't come from us. We can't take any credit. But we can enjoy watching the transformation happen in the lives of those around whom we've been planted.

Small Things with Love

Mother Theresa is a name recognized by most people throughout the world. Born in Albania, Mary Teresa Bojaxhiu migrated to Ireland to join the Sisters of Loreto and train to become a missionary. During her time within that order, she received the call from God to leave the convent and serve the poor while living among them. She spent the rest of her life caring for those who were infected with leprosy and close to death, the poorest of the poor.

There is a quote commonly attributed to Mother Teresa: "Don't look for big things. Just do small things with love. The smaller the thing, the greater must be our love."

Sometimes we are guilty of thinking so big that we miss the small opportunities immediately in front of us. Not many people can fly overseas and serve the poor and dying in Calcutta. Not many can give up their nine-to-five jobs to go into full-time ministry. Some people can do these things — which is fantastic — but most cannot. Indeed, most are not called by God to those places.

Just as there was only one Mother Theresa, there is only one you. No matter what set of circumstances, giftings, or passions you carry, God wants to use you to bless your little part of the world. May God give us grace to love those around us—to do "small things with great love."

When Jesus spoke about the end of the age and his return, he said this:

> Then the King will say to those on his right, "Come, you who are blessed by my Father, inherit the Kingdom prepared for you from the creation of the world. For I was hungry, and you fed me. I was thirsty, and you gave me a drink. I was a stranger, and you invited me into your home. I was naked, and you gave me clothing. I was sick, and you cared for me. I was in prison, and you visited me." (Matthew 25:35-36)

Notice what is on this list. Feeding someone hungry. Welcoming the stranger into your home. Meeting the basic needs of others around you. Caring for the sick. Lifting the burden of loneliness by taking time to be present with someone else. This is what matters to God.

You get God's attention by noticing the needs that are in front of you—and taking action. He values the things that are done for him in secret and simplicity, apart from a stage or a trending Instagram post. It's all about the small things. The kind word. The act of compassion. They are *doable* acts of love, which require no degree, no platform, no permission. These are the tiny actions that transform lives. Never underestimate the power of simple acts of love.

> Then these righteous ones will reply, "Lord, when did we ever see you hungry and feed you? Or thirsty and give you something to drink? Or a stranger and show you hospitality? Or naked and give you clothing? When did we ever see you sick or in prison and visit you?' And the King will say, 'I tell you the truth, when you did it to one of the least of these my brothers and sisters, you were doing it to me"! (Matthew 25:37-40)

God is not looking for a few talented people to do epic things for him. He is looking for all his children to be authentic, intentional, and consistent in loving the people right in front of them, one at a time.

This is God's upside-down kingdom. You make an impact by thinking small, not by seeking a stage. You gain his attention by loving the "least of these" in a way that no one else may ever see. This is what earns the applause of heaven. This is the Jesus way. "As the Father has sent me, I am sending you" (John 20:21).

I can take time to listen to my neighbor, to *really* understand them. I can bake cookies. I can change the oil in someone's car. I can help somebody move. I can shovel a driveway. I can mow a lawn. I can pick up the phone and call.

These small acts of love make a difference. Each conversation, each interaction demonstrates that a person has value. It is love that opens up the heart. And, if that weren't enough, when we do it for the "least of these," we do it for him (Matthew 25:40).

Kindness Trumps Love

Condemnation and shame never changed anyone for the better. Instead, it is "the kindness of God leads us to repentance" (Romans 2:4 NASB). Mysteriously, it's the gentle nature in Jesus—expressed in his tenderness and unwavering commitment to us—that woos our hearts. It causes us to think about ourselves in a different light and produces a shift in our hearts.

The Church in the West doesn't have a reputation for being kind. We have been characterized as judgmental, condescending, and lacking compassion. While this may be an unfair generalization, it is certainly something we need to guard against. But how?

There is a difference between love and kindness. Love has become such a cheap word. I use that same word to express my preference for brownies, my commitment to my wife, and my devotion to God. A person can be critical of someone and yet claim, "I'm just showing them tough love." It's a word that has been emptied of meaning.

Kindness, however, still carries some potency. You can't be critical of your neighbor and still claim to be kind. It is accompanied by gentleness. It is sincere. It reserves judgment for another time and place—or shuts it down altogether. It refuses to crush others with sarcasm or judgment, even if in the moment you feel you are justified in doing so. It makes allowances for the immaturity or rough edges in others.

The word itself pulls back the facade, exposing the true motives of our hearts. Kindness comes with no strings attached.

What would happen if we were intentional about being kind before being right? What if Christians were known for extravagant kindness rather than our stance on political agendas? Perhaps then, our social media posts would be worth reading!

At first, our tendency may be to fear that if we resort to kindness, then people will never change. That we must be hard on them, that we have a moral duty to point out the errors in their lives. All the while, we forget God has adopted a "kindness first" policy as he relates to us.

> Since you judge others for doing these things, why do you think you can avoid God's judgment when you do the same things? Don't you see how wonderfully kind, tolerant, and patient God is with you? Does this mean nothing to you? Can't you see that his kindness is intended to turn you from your sin? (Romans 2:3-4)

Mother Teresa once said: "Spread love everywhere you go. First of all, in your house. Give love to your children, to your wife or husband, to a next-door neighbor. Let no one ever come to you without leaving better and happier. Be the living expression of God's kindness. Kindness in your face, kindness in your eyes, kindness in your smile."[13]

Many people have said no to "Guilt Jesus," to "Demanding Jesus," and to "Critical Jesus." These counterfeits lead no one into freedom. They point out the apparent struggles people have but offer no solutions. It's time for Jesus' followers to be intentionally kind to all. As we reflect God's love to people, we'll begin to see real transformation. An invitation is being extended to us to clarify what God is like to a lost and hurting world.

Get Full, Then Spill

In Acts 3, Peter and John are going to the Temple to take part in a time of prayer. Along the way, they see a man who can't walk. He is begging for money. "Peter and John looked at him intently, and Peter said, 'Look at us!' The lame man looked at them eagerly, expecting some money. But Peter said, 'I don't have any silver or gold for you. But I'll give you what I have. In the name of Jesus Christ, the Nazarene, get up and walk!'" (Acts 3:4-6).

This story illustrates a simple but profound principle: What you have, you can give. What you *don't* have, you *cannot* give. Peter and John weren't wealthy. They couldn't fix the man's financial problems, but they carried something else that was real and very potent. It was that "special sauce" coming from the Holy Spirit, nurtured in the secret place, and birthed with a faith that effectively said, "In this moment, Jesus is more than enough for you."

Before you step out to love your neighbor, make sure you are carrying something inside. Back in the day, those in the Church called this "anointing" or an "unction." This is not something you can produce on your own. It's the Holy Spirit producing His fruit in your life. And you don't need much to make an impact.

Jesus shared how those who believed in him should come to him and "drink" or receive from him. This would produce "rivers of living water [that] will flow from his heart" (John 7:38). God intends for you to be someone who overflows with his presence. But the only way to get filled up is by spending time with him and intentionally receiving his love for you.

Answering the call to step out and love your neighbor can be terrifying. When you position yourself as the giver, you quickly find out whether you have something to give. Action strips away the flowery language and neatly packaged ideas. Do you *actually* have something to offer?

I think of how my younger kids get water when it's time for dinner. I go to the sink and fill up my glass three-quarters of the way full. It's the sensible thing to do. Why? I want to make sure as I'm walking from the sink to my table that I don't spill anything on the floor.

My younger boys have their own way. They place their cups under the water faucet and fill it to the very top. The water practically leans over the edge of the glass, ready to spill. It doesn't take much imagination to guess what happens on their way back to the table. There's water everywhere!

It's my joy to wake up early and spend the quiet moments of the morning with a cup of coffee in one hand and my Bible in the other. I read God's Word; then I pray God's Word. And then I hear him speak to my heart. These simple motions have this mysterious effect of filling me up. I do it regularly because, as we talked about earlier in the book, I "leak." But when you're full, you can't help but spill some of what you have onto those around you.

You were designed by God to spill love on people wherever you go. "He uses us to spread the knowledge of Christ everywhere, like a sweet perfume" (2 Corinthians 2:14). All that's required of any of us is to just show up—again and again—in his presence. As you make space for God in your life, before too long, you'll discover yourself "spilling out" wherever you go.

I went to a pretty traditional church as a young man. Everyone would get dressed up. As my family entered the front door, there would be older men and women ready to welcome us. I always tried to avoid being greeted by the older ladies. They were sweet, but they wore an inexcusable amount of perfume. I think as they aged, their noses lost some sensitivity. So to compensate, they would spritz extra perfume all over themselves.

They would catch me hiding behind my parents and draw me close and give me a hug. For the rest of the day, their perfume would be all over me. I would go home and change my clothes, yet the smell lingered. Only by showering and changing clothes could I get any relief!

While being stuck with the lingering scents of someone else's perfume is an unpleasant reality we've all experienced, it illustrates a point. When you are full of something, especially when you are full of God, it just spills out. And it has a residual effect — it lingers.

Position yourself regularly in God's presence. Be intentional to receive. Then get out there and start spilling God's kindness over the ones he puts in your path. His love is all you can carry, and, fortunately, it's precisely what the world needs.

It's Just Like Fishing

Last summer, I took my family camping. We went to a state park that was well-known for trout fishing. It's a bit ironic, actually, because I don't know how to fish. We loaded up all our fishing gear and headed out to the river. I had bought all types of lures: squishy, shiny, pointy. I felt well equipped for the simple task at hand.

An hour into our fishing expedition, my kids became suspicious. *Maybe Dad doesn't really know everything.* Not a single bite. I could swear I heard the fish mocking me from the riverbank. I was ready to give up.

At just that moment, a young lady came over and told us we were using the wrong bait. She opened a small jar of PowerBait® designed explicitly for trout. She gave me about a tablespoon worth of the bright, tacky substance. I held it like gold in my hands as she told me, "Don't use a lot. A little goes a long way."

That small gift changed everything. Within twenty minutes, my five-year-old son caught four trout, and another of my boys nabbed the fifth. That trip taught me that you don't need to be an expert to catch fish — you just need the right bait. That evening we enjoyed one of the most amazing meals I've ever cooked over a campfire.

There are people all around us who are desperate for love. At its best, all this world can provide is a counterfeit, knockoff version of the acceptance and kindness offered by God. This world system has a reputation for over-promising and under-delivering. When it comes to God's love, you don't need much to make a difference. You don't need to be an expert. "A little goes a long way."

The next morning, we went back to the same spot where we had been fishing. We had our special bait. We had our lines out in the water. In my engineering mind, I'm expecting a repeat of the day before. Same variables. Same results. We couldn't catch any fish.

Then came the next lesson: Having the right bait is only part of the equation; you still have to go to where the fish are. The same principle is true for loving others. You must go to where they are.

Don't become so insulated from the rest of the world that you overlook people who are hurting and hungry and needing love. They are all around you—I promise. Walk around your neighborhood in the evening. Go to Starbucks and drink your coffee without your eyes glued to a phone. Have lunch with your coworkers. Take time to get to know people.

Following Jesus is less about getting it right and more about moving in the right direction. God values movement. Simply live the life you have been given, being kind wherever you go, and rest assured that "you will always harvest what you plant" (Galatians 6:7). It will come naturally. It won't feel forced.

> **FOLLOWING JESUS IS LESS ABOUT GETTING IT RIGHT AND MORE ABOUT MOVING IN THE RIGHT DIRECTION.**

Jesus said, "I have been given all authority in heaven and on earth. Therefore, go…" (Matthew 28:18-19). The default to GO. Assume every light is green. Shift your gears into drive and keep moving until Jesus shows you otherwise. You have permission to love the person in front of you. You are released to be Jesus to them. Don't hold back.

Love Takes Time

No farmer plants a single seed in preparation for a future harvest. There are variables beyond his control. He overcomes those unknown obstacles by scattering seed far and wide (Mark 4:26). And only God knows which seed will fall into good soil. The farmer's job, and yours, is to scatter seed.

God is the one who causes the growth. So be extravagant in your love. Love often and indiscriminately. You may see a steaming pile with a putrid stench, but God sees soil enriched with fertilizer. Often the most unattractive and hopeless situations produce the best crop.

There's an older man my wife and I have known and loved for seven years. We met Jon when we moved into an older home on the east side of Saint Paul. He lived in the rundown apartment building next door. Jon had lived a full life: military service, drug abuse, living in artistic communities like Slab City, and making annual trips to Burning Man. In the twilight of his life, he was living in isolation from everyone except his tiny dog, Scrappy.

The first Christmas we were there, we threw a party for the neighborhood and invited Jon. He was cynical and only seemed to be partly there. Years of LSD usage had scrambled his compass on reality. While we had some very interesting conversations at our table, it was heartbreaking to see the world of loneliness and confusion in which he lived.

Over the years we lived in that home, we looked for every opportunity to love Jon. There was always a seat at the dinner table for him. We threw him birthday parties. Perhaps one of the only benefits of his isolation was that he was always available. We unofficially adopted him—without his permission. As long as he didn't tell us to stop, we were determined to be love to him.

The change wasn't visible for quite some time. When Jon came over, he brought his brokenness with him. He spoke about God as a puppet master and life as a "sick joke." He thought he was stuck inside a reality like *The Matrix*. Jon was testing us, and rightfully so. He had been let down by so many.

When it felt appropriate, we shared with him about Jesus — little bite-sized morsels. It was like trying to pour water into a two-liter bottle. The opening was tiny, so we needed precision. We felt like most of our love was missing the opening and just making a mess on the floor. Many times we even asked ourselves, "What are we doing?" But love is never wasted.

Slowly, he began to love us. He'd call with ideas for art projects for the kids. Once, he bought markers and notebooks for the boys. He gave out of the little he had. I recognized a major shift one night after dinner, when he said, "I love you guys, too." We had finally won him over. He received our love and was able to give his in return. He loved us before he loved Jesus, and I think that's actually a good approach to follow.

Three years ago, we moved to the country. We said our goodbyes to Jon and shared some weepy moments. But we've stayed in touch; we had become friends, after all. A few months ago, we stopped by his house and discovered he had decided to follow Jesus. He shared matter-of-factly how he had been listening to Christian radio. He emphatically told us, "Yeah, I'm a believer now." We were shocked! Jon is no longer just part of my family, he's been adopted into God's family.

Meaningful growth most often occurs in hidden places. You plant a seed in the ground. The rain waters it. The sun warms the soil. And all the while, it seems as if nothing is happening. We may even be tempted to give up hope. But then, when we least expect it, the plant bursts forth from the ground.

Keep in mind that person — your neighbor or coworker or grocery store clerk — was valuable enough to God for him to send His Son for them. If they were worth the most precious gift that could be given, then most certainly, they are worth the investment of your time.

God calculates his return on investment differently than we do. We need to stop trying to change the entire world and instead begin loving the people in front of us. Waste your life loving others, loving simply, loving practically. Allow God to worry about the return.

> The Kingdom of God is like a farmer who scatters seed on the ground. Night and day, while he's asleep or awake, the seed sprouts and grows, but he does not understand how it happens. The earth produces the crops on its own. First a leaf blade pushes through, then the heads of wheat are formed, and finally the grain ripens. And as soon as the grain is ready, the farmer comes and harvests it with a sickle, for the harvest time has come. (Mark 4:26).

The growing piece is a mystery to us, and it takes time. But for something to grow, a seed must be planted. And seeds are only planted on purpose. Intentional love, spread indiscriminately wherever we go, is the best fertilizer for the harvest.

God invites us to partner with him in loving those who are in front of us. The Holy Spirit who dwells in you eagerly wants to get out and reach those around you. Respond to the invitation. Join the adventure. Have fun and discover the joy that can be found in loving without strings attached.

Apply

Growth requires change. It's that simple. Throughout nature, we see the old adage proved true again and again: "If nothing changes, nothing changes." Every songbird has been pushed out of its nest. It's the only way its newly discovered wings can be put to use. All it takes is a little bit of courage and a nudge. The same is true for us. Through inward reflection, we discover our "wings," but it's only by application that we learn to fly.

Several suggestions for applying the truths from this chapter have been included below. This is not an exhaustive list. However, it should be enough to get you started. Find something that fits your personality. It should be action-oriented and push you just a little further than you feel comfortable.

- Spend a few minutes in quiet reflection, thinking about the people you encounter regularly. Don't only think about your friends. For example, include your neighbors, that quiet coworker at the office, or the barista at the local coffee shop. Ask the Holy Spirit to highlight two or three of those people who could benefit from receiving God's love. Write down their names in the space below as a reminder.

_____

_____

_____

_____

_____

_____

_____

- John Wesley, a powerful preacher and missionary from the 1700s, once said, "God does nothing except in response to believing prayer." Prayer is a powerful tool! You can bring about change in the lives of others. Begin praying every day for those people on your list. You may find it helpful to use some of the sample prayers below.

- Father, draw _____ to yourself (John. 6:44).
- Give _____ a heart that is softened and responsive to your goodness (Ezekiel 11:19).
- Help _____ to see him/herself the way you see them, as having value and being loved (Jeremiah 31:3).
- Give _____ a desire to know you (Acts 17:27).

- As you pray for these people, you will discover God gives you the ability to see them the way he sees them. You will notice your heart feeling differently toward them. In parallel to this practice, look for something you can do to express kindness to them without the expectation of receiving anything in return. For example, if you're a good baker, then bake them some cookies. Take your coworker out for lunch. Look for opportunities to live a lifestyle of unexpected and undeserved kindness.

- If you feel comfortable, spend some time in prayer, asking the Holy Spirit, "How do you see this person? What in them is especially precious to you?" Write down your impressions on a small piece of paper or a notecard. If you're unsure of what you wrote down, you can share it with someone else who follows Jesus and knows how to hear his voice. Focus on words that will be encouraging. Don't overthink it. When the time is right, share the card with them. Try not to be weird. The goal is to express God's love for them, not to "get them saved" or make them a project. Show them simple and authentic kindness.

CONCLUSION

We have reached the final pages of this book. However, rather than finding "the end," what lies ahead is the beginning of a new chapter, one to be experienced not through paper and ink, but through the mountains and valleys of real life. Now comes the opportunity to practice and to find in the midst of it all an expanded grace to respond to God's invitation.

This book was not written to educate, but rather to facilitate a connection — or, in some cases, a reconnection — with the God who has been following you all your life. He is the one who chose you before the foundation of the world was laid (Ephesians 1:4). You have been seen, called out, and pursued. Quite honestly, you could not ask for better circumstances in which to respond.

This book is not for those who think they are strong or wise or capable. I've written to ordinary people like myself, those who have questions and doubts, but who also dare to embrace mystery and turn toward Jesus rather away from him. He can be felt within, calling out to you, his voice echoing in the chambers of your soul.

The principles in this book must be learned and relearned, moment by moment, reaching ever deeper into the lowest places of our souls. It is my hope that these words have helped to demystify and bring clarity to what it looks like to enjoy a relationship with God. Above all, I aim to leave you with hope, thinking, "Yes, I think I can give this a try."

Reflection sections crafted for each chapter were designed to make you turn inward and consider the state of your soul. With the rate of change in the world today, and how quickly we grow, you'll likely need to return back to those questions regularly. You'll need to connect with the Holy Spirit through prayer and ask him to search your heart and show you what lies within. You may be surprised at what you find.

Application sections provided examples, showing you how the truths in each chapter might be put into practice. It's my hope that you found at least some of the examples relevant to you in this present season. You may find other application exercises stand out later, especially as you enter a different season of life. Follow the life-giving paths, those that connect you with the presence of the One who has called you.

This is a book of tools, but tools only benefit you in so much as you choose to use them — and use them correctly! So I'm challenging you to put the principles into practice. Try and fail. Try and fail. Again and again. Practice them until they are second nature.

It's very much like making it to the end of a manual for a ten-speed bicycle. The last page has been read, and now it is time to ride and feel the wind in your face. Occasionally you'll need to hit the brakes and slow down. There will be times when you hit a pothole or get a flat tire. You will certainly need to make repairs and adjustments along the way. The manual is only the introduction to a lifelong adventure. The time has come to move!

The Promise

This book began with a promise that following Jesus can be doable for the ordinary person. It's not limited to the saints of old or those who seemed to have been especially gifted or who are just in the right place at the right time. We admire these people for their dedication, but they were just like us.

I'm convinced that they actually felt quite ordinary. And it was not until many years later, as others reflected on their lives, that it was discovered just how spectacular the sum of their lives had become.

I would encourage you to believe that your daily commitment to follow Jesus, even now in the mundane comings and goings of life, is precious in the eyes of God. This includes those moments no one will see. Those thoughts no one will know. Those deeds no one will discover. They have not gone unnoticed. The Father sees it all and is, even at this moment, issuing a fresh invitation to respond to him.

My Invitation

This book exists because of God's invitation to me. The lessons found in these pages have come from him, from years of deposits made into my heart. There were many times over the years when I turned down his invitation. But God never gave up on me. And in those times when I finally gave in and opened my stubborn heart, he was always there waiting to meet with me.

Reflecting back on these chapters, I understand now what the Apostle John wrote later in his life: "We proclaim to you what we ourselves have actually seen and heard so that you may have fellowship with us. And our fellowship is with the Father and with his Son, Jesus Christ" (1 John 1:3). I'm giving to you that which I have received from the Father. In fact, that is all I have to give that is worth much of anything. You now hold in your hands what I have received from him.

God's invitation, his calling out to me, has always remained constant. It came to me long before I even understood it. True to his nature, he's always the initiator, the One who goes before us to prepare the way. When I first became aware of him and his invitation, I was a child and had nothing to give him. It came again to me as a young man who was full of passion and doubts and questions.

God reached out in times of success when I was tempted to trust in my strength rather than his. He has called out to me during my failures — which have been many. And, in fact, it is perhaps during those times of failure that I have heard his call all the more clearly. And I expect that tomorrow morning when I rise, whether I perceive it or not, his call will be there.

His invitation has always remained, unaffected by success or failure, without regard for good deeds done or bad deeds avoided. His invitation has always been present, along with his hand extended to me and his voice speaking to my heart: "Get up. Let's try again. Let's do this together!" His voice, always kind and hopeful, has inspired and sustained me through the years.

I've been caught in his magnetic field, pulled toward him by unseen hands. And just like a magnet drawing a piece of metal towards it, he's the one with the special properties. May God give us the grace to see that we are all caught in his magnetic field. His call is extended to all, and he is actively engaged in drawing us toward himself. The real question is whether you will welcome the draw, or whether you will resist it. My question to you, in the final pages of this book, is how will you respond to his magnetic invitation?

Your Invitation

This book traveled from my heart into your hands. But has it passed from your hands into your heart? As it has been said by many, "The longest journey you will ever take is the eighteen inches from your head to your heart." The words in this book indeed are only as valuable as they are practiced.

So don't be in a rush to finish this book. Put it on your shelf, but return to it often. Not because my words are particularly memorable, but rather because they stand as an opportunity to enter into conversation with God, who is the truly spectacular one.

Don't judge yourself by your failures or weaknesses. It is consistent action, small steps, movements in the mundane, that really matter. They add up into something marvelous, but it takes time. There are no shortcuts to growing in God. But each step is worth it. Each step produces value, whether you perceive it or not.

Their Invitation

This book traveled from my heart into your hands. Perhaps it's traveled from your hands into your heart. And now, the final step is that it might pass from your heart into someone else's hands. If this book has impacted your heart, I want to ask you to place this book in someone else's hands.

You and I have walked together through these pages, as I have shared my story. I want to encourage you to walk with somebody else and to share your story, or to team up with others and journey together. I would love to hear about your stories. You can do that by leaving me a review on Amazon or by visiting my web site.

The Last Bits

The invitation has gone out. The call has been sounded. A decision must be made. As a friend of mine once said, "Jesus is not looking for fans, he's looking for followers." How will you respond?

May the Father give you grace
to perceive and to respond
to the invitation he has extended to you.

May the Son open your ears
to hear his gentle voice within
that you may follow joyfully in his steps.

May the Holy Spirit empower you
to never give up and to never stop looking
for the adventures that remain to be discovered.

This is but the first step.

Amen.

HOW TO SUBMIT A BOOK REVIEW

Wait! I have one final request. It's hard to make an impact as a new author. Book reviews are a powerful way to provide me with feedback and help spread the word. Would you be willing to take two minutes and provide some feedback? I love five-star reviews, but I also appreciate honesty. Submit your honest (and kind) reviews using this link: www.themattberry.com/book-review. Thanks!

Endnotes

1 Bonhoeffer, Dietrich. The Cost of Discipleship. New York: Touchstone, 1995, p. 44.

2 Tozer, A.W. The Knowledge of the Holy. New York: HarperOne, 1978, p. 1.

3 Tozer, A.W. The Pursuit of Man. Camp Hill: Christian Publications, 1978, p. 13.

4 Scripture clearly indicates that believers receive the Holy Spirit at the moment of conversion (see 1 Corinthians 12:13, Ephesians 1:13, Romans 8:9). If you have decided to follow Jesus, you have the Holy Spirit. Period. Nothing more must be done to "get" him. Yet, there is also the reality of receiving or welcoming him in to occupy more areas of our lives. That is a gradual process that we "walk out" daily. It requires intentionality. As we learn to trust him and make space for him in our lives, he fills us in a greater way—again and again. The invitation for us, and the goal for which I seek, is that one day there will be no place in my heart (i.e., opinions about others, relationships, thought life, etc.) in which he does not have an "unlocked door." May God give you grace to provide him with access to come and make beauty in your life.

5 O'Neill, Robert. The Operator. New York: Scribner, 2017, p. 49.

6 Brother Lawrence, The Practice of the Presence of God. New Kensington: Whitaker House, 1982. Digital.

7 Virkler, Mark. 4 Keys to Hearing God's Voice. Shippensburg: Destiny Image Publishers, 2010, p. 100.

8 Chambers, Oswald. Prayer: A Holy Occupation. Grand Rapids: Discovery House Publishers, 2010, p. 61.

9 "trust." Merriam-Webster.com. Merriam-Webster, 2020. Web. 1 Apr 2020.

10 Swindoll, Charles. "Attitude." December 2, 2003, Dallas Theological Seminary, YouTube, https://www.youtube.com/watch?v=9lnvN0buts4.

11 Liddell, Eric. The Disciplines of the Christian Life. Escondido: Abingdon Press, 1985, What Is Discipleship?

12 Zwemer, S.M. The Solitary Throne London: Pickering and Inglis, 1937), p. 1.

13 Douglas, J.D. Let the Earth Hear His Voice. Minneapolis: World Wide Publications, 1975, p. 25.

ABOUT MATT BERRY

Matt Berry is an author and director of The Jesus Following Network. He also works full-time in the field of Cybersecurity. His mission in life is to inspire and nurture a lifestyle of movement, freedom, and rest in the lives of spiritually inclined people. He and his wife, Elisa, live in Big Lake, Minnesota, where they are raising their four boys to be world changers—and to not burp at the table.

To receive updates on upcoming books and free resources, visit www.themattberry.com/signup

To inquire about having Matt speak at your event, visit www.themattberry.com/bookings

THE JESUS FOLLOWING

The Jesus Following Network is a missional community pursuing change in the church and transformation in the world. We are a tribe of ordinary people seeking to follow Jesus in ways that are practical, sustainable, and easy to multiply. We exist to shift paradigms, awaken dreams, and empower Jesus followers to be "on mission" with him right where they are planted. As this occurs, we expect to see God's kingdom revealed in the everyday spaces of life.

Along the way, we developed a tool that has become useful for having Jesus-focused conversations. This tool, which we call a *Growth Group*, has been used by those who are intentionally following Jesus and those who are still seeking. It brings together some of the most important ingredients for spiritual growth: inward reflection, reading Scripture, and prayer for others. Find out more at www.jesusfollowing.com/growth-groups.

For more information about The Jesus Following Network, visit
www.jesusfollowing.com

Made in the USA
Monee, IL
03 December 2020

50680500R00135